THE CROWN, THE NOBILITY
AND THE PEASANTS
1630–1713

Antti Kujala

THE CROWN,
THE NOBILITY AND
THE PEASANTS
1630–1713

Tax, rent and relations of power

SKS / Finnish Literature Society
Helsinki 2003

Studia Historica 69

Cover: King Charles XI receiving the declaration by the estates on the mode of government in 1680. Lithograph by M. Neuhaus. National Board of Antiquities.

Back cover: The coat of arms of the counts of Vasaborg. National Board of Antiquities.

Keywords: Sweden/Finland – social history – taxes – power relations – 1630–1713

www.finlit.fi

ISBN 951-746-473-8
ISSN 0081-6493

Vammalan Kirjapaino Oy
Vammala 2003

CONTENTS

Acknowledgements

The present study was prepared with the aid of two-year project grant from the Academy of Finland. The Finnish-Swedish Cultural Foundation provided a grant for a two-week period of research in Stockholm, and my friend Hannu Säniö kindly gave me lodging there for the third week that I needed to finish my work in the archives. The National Archives of Finland and the National Archives of Sweden provided the necessary archive services. Facilities for work were made possible by the National Archives of Finland and the Department of History of the University of Helsinki. I wish to express my warmest thanks to the above bodies. I express my gratitude to Professor Heikki Ylikangas and Professor Anthony F. Upton for their kind support. I am also indebted to Senior Inspector Matti Walta of the Finnish National Archives, Oula Silvennoinen, who was my research assistant for a six-month period, to Jüri Kokkonen for translating the study into English, to Arttu Paarlahti, who drew the maps, and to Rauno Enden of the Finnish Literature Society who was instrumental in arranging the publication of this book.

Antti Kujala

To Pirjo

Sweden during the period of dominion

The 17th century was Sweden's period of dominion as a leading European power. It came to an end in the Peace of Nystad in 1721, in connection with which Russia took Sweden's former role as the leading nation of Northern Europe.

Already in the Middle Ages, Sweden had conquered Finland and integrated it to be part of the kingdom. The later territorial conquests in the Baltic lands and Germany partly retained their own institutions and administration, thus remaining outside Sweden and Finland, the core area of the realm. Estonia was annexed to the Kingdom of Sweden in the 1560s, followed in 1617 by Ingermanland (Ingria) and the Province of Kexholm which were conquered from Russia. In 1595 the northern end of Finland's eastern border had already been moved from the Gulf of Bothnia to the shore of the Arctic Ocean, a loss to Russia. In practice, Sweden had no longer respected the old border for quite some time. A long war with Poland ended in 1629 with Swedish rule over Livonia. The focus of Swedish foreign policy and expansions shifted from the northeastern parts of the Baltic Sea area first to the southeast and finally to the south. In 1630 King Gustavus II Adolphus (1611–1632) intervened in the Thirty Years' War by sending his army to Germany. Swedish foreign policy was a mixture of defensiveness and expansionism, which was also associated with the tendency to dominate the Baltic. The Thirty Years' War was also a war of religion, but Lutheran Sweden took part in the war as a paid ally and in the assistance of Catholic France. In the Peace of Westphalia in 1648, Sweden

The old church of Nystad, built in the late 1620s, repaired and thoroughly restored in the 18th century. The bell tower was added in 1775. Nystad was founded in 1617 to attract the unregulated seafaring and trading of the peasants to the town to profit the crown and the town burghers. The Peace Treaty of Nystad was signed in 1721 in this little town which had suffered the hardships of war, exhausting most of its drive and activity of the previous century. Photo: A. Kujala.

annexed the dioceses of Bremen and Verden, parts of Pomerania and the town of Wismar.

Throughout this period, however, Denmark (Denmark-Norway) was Sweden's worst competitor, having forced severe reparations upon Sweden in two wars, first in the 1560s and later in the 1610s. In 1645 the roles were reversed and Denmark ceded Ösel (Saaremaa), Gotland, Jämtland, Härjedalen and Halland (the latter for 30 years) to Sweden

Charles X Gustav (1654–1660) was at war at the same time against Poland, Denmark and Russia. The king's invasion of Poland

and prolonged military campaign there ended with the death of the warrior king and the recognition of the status quo. A similar solution was reached in the treaty concluded with Russia. On the other hand, the king managed to subdue Denmark completely, the latter having to cede Skåne (Scania), one of the most important areas of the kingdom to Sweden, as well as the provinces of Blekinge, Halland and Bohuslän. Unlike the conquered territories on the other side of the Baltic, the former Danish provinces were integrated into the Kingdom of Sweden.

Sweden was a poor country with a small population and an agrarian economy. It was able, however, to obtain considerable revenue from the export of copper and iron. The nobility was the leading class, or estate, of society, but it was unable to control its peasants or society to the same degree as in many other European countries. The peasants mostly remained free. The *Riksdag*, composed of four estates, had the right to participate in legislation alongside the monarch and in the aid of the latter. The monarchs naturally used the *Riksdag* to commit and bind society to decisions, by no means least to new taxes. Alongside the nobility, the clergy, burghers and peasants were represented in the riksdag. The *Riksdag* represented only the core areas of the realm, i.e. Sweden and Finland; there were no representatives from the conquered territories.

The Swedish crown efficiently mobilized the scant resources of a poor society. The reformed central administration, provincial administration and the judiciary kept the wheels in motion. The taxation of the peasants was taken to such extremes in the 1620s that there was no longer any leeway for raising taxes. In the conscriptions that were carried out with the blessing of the *Riksdag*, the crown obtained the soldiers that it needed for its wars with the cooperation of the peasantry. The authorities primarily sought to recruit soldiers from among the landless population, but also land-owning peasants were conscripted. Owing to its efficient government administration and social order, Sweden could successfully wage war against larger and stronger countries and beat Denmark, which was roughly its equal but had for long been economically more powerful. Recent historical research in Sweden and Finland has discussed the question of whether the great efficiency of the Swedish crown and Swedish society in relation to limited resources was primarily due to coercion or to decision-making relying on broad-based participation and consensus.

Paradoxically, concluding peace became more expensive for the Swedish crown than the war, the costs of which were passed on to the inhabitants of the foreign theatre of war or were funded by France. When peace was concluded, the crown had to redeem its financial obligations. In the years following the Peace of Westphalia, Queen Christina (reigned 1644–1654) donated large numbers of peasant farms or, more precisely, their crown taxes to be collected by the military commanders and her favourites. The costs of generous donations and the reduction of crown revenue were borne in the war against Denmark and Brandenburg in the late 1670s. King Charles XI (1672–1697) was barely able to repel Denmark seeking to avenge its losses, and a small part of Pomerania had to be given to Brandenburg. The crisis of Sweden's state economy and the relatively poor success of the armed forces proved to the king that the policy favouring the nobles had run its course and he put the blame for everything on the regency of high-ranking nobles that had governed while he was still a minor.

In 1680, Charles began a restitution in which the vast majority of the taxes donated to the nobles were restored to being collected by the crown. At the same time, Sweden adopted autocratic rule. The allotment system made it possible to direct the majority of crown taxes directly into the salaries of soldiers. The system was static and prone to disturbances, but it functioned well in peacetime conditions. The armed forces were organized on a basis that was more permanent and regular than conscription. As a result Sweden was better prepared for war than ever before when King Charles XI died in 1697.

Until the end of his life, the king managed to keep Sweden out of wars. The nobility was allowed to keep their formerly owned hereditary land predating the tax donations. Restitution

Queen Christina of Sweden (1644–1654) in the Finnish-language Bible of 1642, represented as the underage ruler still confessing the Evangelic-Lutheran religion prevalent in the kingdom. Drawing by J. Neander and S. Vogel. Not able to combine the demands of her own personality, gender and the crown, Christina finally abdicated. She left Sweden and disclosed her conversion to Catholicism. Library of Borgå Lyceum. Photo: Studio Lignell.

gave the civil-service nobility more regular salaried income than previously and the peasants were freed of the hated practice of conscription. The king carried out the reforms from above, but with the passive support of significant sectors of society. As long as there was peace, the benefits that had been gained were not placed under risk.

Although King Charles XII (1697–1718) dedicated himself completely to serving the god of war, he did not begin the Great Northern War (1700–1721). Instead, Sweden bore the brunt of aggression on the part of its neighbours Denmark, Russia and Poland (initially only its Saxon king). Despite major victories in the field of battle, the king could not subdue Poland any more than Russia, and ultimately remained the losing party in the conflict with the latter. The war destroyed – one at a time – the benefits gained by Swedish society and its estates. Reluctance towards the war permeated the whole of society, including the Privy Council. King Charles, however, kept Sweden at war until he fell in battle in 1718. In the ensuing peace treaties Sweden ceded to Russia Karelia including Viborg, Ingermanland, Estonia, Ösel and Livonia. It also relinquished most of its conquered German territories. The victims of the war included not only the role of a leading power but also autocracy, which was replaced after the death of King Charles by the rule of the (higher) estates.

INTRODUCTION

TAXATION AS A FORM OF EXERCISING POWER

In the preface of *People Meet the Law*, a collection of studies published in 2000, Eva Österberg and Erling Sandmo discuss, among other things, the different approaches with which the Nordic states of the beginning of Modern Time have been reviewed. They reject the idea of a power state or military state based on the subordination of subjects and suggest instead the "negotiating state". The crown negotiated with the local community and its subjects not only via the judiciary but also through collecting taxes.[1] *People Meet the Law* deals with judicial practice and the reference to taxation is made only in passing. In the Nordic countries contemporary ideas of the interaction of the state and its subjects have evolved mainly through studies of the judiciary. There is thus reason to see how well they apply to another important sector of society, viz. taxation.

In discussing 17th-century taxation we cannot bypass the widespread donated-land system whereby the main part of crown taxes from certain peasant holdings was given to nobles as compensation for services rendered to the realm and the regent. In the so-called grand restitution that began to be implemented

---

[1] Eva Österberg & Erling Sandmo, 'Introduction,' *People Meet the Law*, E. Österberg & S. Sogner (eds) (Otta, 2000), pp. 14–15, 22–24.

in the early 1680s most of the donated taxes were restored as crown revenue.[2]

We must thus ask what opportunities the peasants had to influence their own position as subjects of the nobility on the one hand, and the crown on the other. Their ability to manage under the patronage of the nobility and the crown is reviewed mainly at the level of taxation and other cameral-based obligations (labour services or corvée) but also at the level of the real economy. The latter is considerably more difficult, because sources on the economic activities of the nobility cover only relatively small geographic areas and sectors of the economy, while the crown sources are predominantly cameral and are not directly related to the real economy. The position of the peasants in the real economy can be approached, however, particularly with reference to the 1690s and the following decade. Was the peasant thus a mere powerless subject to the power wielded by a noble landlord or the centralized state, or could he influence the forms of this exercise of power and thus improve his own position?

A POWER STATE OR INTERACTION?

According to the English Marxist historian Perry Anderson, the absolutism, the concentration of power in the hands of the monarchy, that came about in Western Europe in the 16th century marked a fundamental change in medieval social systems based on the sovereign role of numerous parallel institutes of classes or estates and vassal relationships. The birth of the international political system in Europe also influenced developments leading to absolutism. In order to succeed in the continuous wars of the period, the state had to create for itself a bureaucracy, reinforce and integrate taxation and promote trade. The armed forces were the largest individual item of state expenditure. According to

---

[2]   Eino Jutikkala, *Bonden i Finland genom tiderna* (Helsingfors, 1963), pp. 149–207.

Anderson, absolutism was based on the social domination of the aristocracy and large-scale ownership of land. Absolutism was the machinery by which the extra-economic, politico-legal coercion practised by the landowners was transferred and concentrated into the hands of the state. Its objective was to keep the peasants in their former subordinate position despite the partial disintegration of feudal relations.

For Anderson, autocracy, the concentration of power in the hands of the monarch was only one form of the centralized absolutist state, and generally speaking this state was not able to completely eradicate various privileges and estate-based institutions.[3] It should be noted that in the present context absolutism refers solely to autocracy and not to other forms of the centralized state of Early Modern Times, as I feel that the traditional usage is more precise.

The Soviet historian B. F. Porshnev regarded taxation practised by the absolutist French state in the 17th century as a single, centralized form of feudal rent as opposed to the rents and payments required by individual feudal landlords.[4] His compatriot Aaron Gurevich regarded medieval Norway to have been a special feudal society, where the peasants kept their freedom, but found themselves in a feudal relationship of subordination in relation to the crown (state), whereby the ruling class utilized the economic and human resources of the peasantry.[5]

Sven A. Nilsson presented the concept of the Swedish military state, which created a special apparatus of control in order to compensate for the small population and poverty of the realm. As its instruments, the state employed the church, the armed forces and administration. Control was implemented through

---

[3]   Perry Anderson, *Lineages of the Absolutist State* (London, 1977), in particular pp. 7–59.
[4]   Boris Porchnev, *Les soulèvements populaires en France de 1623 à 1648* (Paris, 1963), pp. 395–396.
[5]   A. Ja. Gurevitsj, 'De frie bønder i det føydale Norge,' *Frihet og føydalisme: Fra sovjetisk forskning i norsk middelalderhistorie*, Steinar Supphellen (ed.) (Oslo, 1977), especially pp. 110–116. The same perspective was also followed in Soviet histories of Norway and Sweden: *Istoriia Norvegii* (Moskva, 1980) & *Istoriia Shvetsii* (Moskva, 1974).

demographic records kept by the church, conscription and taxation.[6]

Another Swedish researcher, Jan Lindegren, created the model of the military or power state, in which the functions of the feudal economy were combined with the military state and the international economic and political system.[7] Lindegren studied production and demography in the North-Swedish parish of Bygdeå in the period 1620–1640, when continuous conscription reduced the population of the parish by as much as 10 percent. The inhabitants of Bygdeå managed to compensate economically for this considerable sapping of resources by increasing the productivity of their labour. Contrary to expectations, society did not collapse. This study presenting the naked power of the military state showed that the common people could even adapt to catastrophic conditions of this order. After the end of the continuous wars between Sweden and its neighbours, this ability to adapt permitted considerable economic and demographic growth in the 18th century.[8]

According to the American scholar Charles Tilly, Sweden was in the European perspective a capital-poor agrarian state where the pattern of state formation was based on coercion maintained by considerable armed forces and the apparatus of government.[9]

The concept of the Swedish military state maintains that the peasants of the period of dominion were subjugated but not necessarily downtrodden to the degree that they could not have undertaken opposition that even led to minor results. This view differs to some degree from the Finnish idea of the power state,

---

6   Sven A. Nilsson, *De stora krigens tid: Om Sverige som militärstat och bondesamhälle* (Uppsala, 1990).

7   Jan Lindegren, 'Den svenska militärstaten 1560–1720,' *Magtstaten i Norden i 1600-tallet og dens sociale konsekvenser*, Erling Ladewig Petersen (ed.) (Odense, 1984), pp. 99–130; Lindegren, 'Maktstatens resurser,' *Skiss till maktstatsprojekt* (Åbo, 1987), pp. 9–28.

8   Jan Lindegren, *Utskrivning och utsugning: Produktion och reproduktion i Bygdeå 1620–1640* (Uppsala, 1980).

9   Charles Tilly, *Coercion, Capital, and European States, AD 990–1992* (Cambridge, MA, 1995), especially pp. 130–137.

which has been represented above all by Heikki Ylikangas. According to Ylikangas, the docility of the peasants of Finland and Sweden in the 17th and 18th centuries was a result of their powerlessness, and in Finland it was caused by the negative outcome of the so-called War of the Clubs 1596—1597, among other reasons. The centralized state with its measures of conscription and severe punishments was too strong an opponent to be openly resisted. Owing to the minor status, the towns could not be allies as was the case in Western Europe. The authority and unity of the state also remained intact. The peasants, however, were able to pursue their matters through official complaints lodged with the *Riksdag* (Diet) and through the judicial process, although Ylikangas regards these as relatively ineffective means.[10] In his view, large sectors of the populace supported the power state in the 17th century as it began to apply increasingly severe punishment, because they felt that more effective and comprehensive legal supervision protected them against the nobility and the officials of the crown in better ways than the previous situation of "might makes right" that had prevailed under insufficient legal control.[11]

In Swedish studies the theme of the power and military state has been countered by the suggestion that the political culture of Sweden at the beginning of Modern Times was based on the interdependence of the state and the peasantry. The power state could not survive unless a relatively large portion of both the elite and the common people recognized it to be legitimate. The traditional ideology called for mutual solidarity. The peaceful interaction of government and the local community was implemented through institutions such as parish meetings and

---

[10]   Heikki Ylikangas, *Mennyt meissä* (Porvoo, 1990), pp. 67, 80–82; Ylikangas, *Klubbekriget: Det blodiga bondekriget i Finland 1596–97* (Stockholm, 1999), passim. See also Ylikangas, 'The Historical Connections of European Peasant Revolts,' *Scandinavian Journal of History* 1991, pp. 85–104.

[11]   Heikki Ylikangas, 'What Happened to Violence?,' *Five Centuries of Violence in Finland and the Baltic Area* (Helsinki, 1998), pp. 7–128.

local court sessions (assizes). Conflict and compromise were two forms of interaction.

Eva Österberg, who has strongly proposed the idea of interaction, readily admits that the crown and the local community were not equal partners, but she also wants to point to the fact that subject could influence the authorities and not only vice-versa. Only the elements of society beneath the peasants (servants and landless rural dwellers) lacked influence.

Österberg wants to underline the freedom of Nordic society instead of the repression that the supporters of the power-state theory have regarded as the prime characteristic of the Swedish state of the beginning of Modern Times. The difference in interpretation thus even gains political overtones. Österberg and many others, however, have taken distance from the theory of the power state also insofar as it entails the idea that the authorities had almost limitless opportunities to steer their subjects from above and that there was hardly any room for the latter to undertake any active or independent measures.[12]

The interaction model inspired Nils Erik Villstrand in his study of the reactions of two local communities in Finland to conscription during the period of dominion. Responses varied from adaptation to protest. At Kalajoki in Ostrobothnia income from tar-burning favoured an adaptive response, with the hiring of substitute soldiers as its main mechanism. In Säminge in Eastern Finland widespread military desertion was a common, yet not the sole strategy to survive the situation.[13]

Petri Karonen regards, in Österberg's terms, a tendency towards peaceful interaction and harmony to have been predominant

---

[12]   Eva Österberg, 'Bönder och centralmakt i det tidigmoderna Sverige: Konflikt – kompromiss – politisk kultur,' Scandia 1989, pp. 73–95. Also, e.g. Johan Söderberg, 'En fråga om civilisering: Brottmål och tvister i svenska häradsrätter 1540–1660,' Historisk Tidskrift 1990, pp. 229–258; Harald Gustafsson, Political Interaction in the Old Regime: Central Power and Local Society in the Eighteenth-Century Nordic States (Lund, 1994).

[13]   Nils Erik Villstrand, Anpassning eller protest: Lokalsamhället inför utskrivningarna av fotfolk till den svenska krigsmakten 1620–1679 (Åbo, 1992).

Harvesting the burn-beaten lands as illustrated by the history book of Olaus Magnus. In the old prosperous areas of Southwest Finland, the farming of arable fields had fully replaced the cultivation of burnt woodlands by the 17th century, but the method was still in occasional use in plots outside the village fields. However, during the first centuries of the modern era the spreading of the population from Savolax both towards the northern and eastern parts of that region and beyond to the west was mostly based on this form of cultivation, i.e., making clearings in the forests, burning the trees thus cut down, and sowing crops in the ashes. Such plots could be harvested only two or three times. Once the land became barren, the farmers had to move on. The people of Savolax also inhabited the Province of Kexholm that had been taken from the Russians, as well as various remote areas in Sweden proper; considered to be "forest rapists", Sweden forced some of them to emigrate to the Swedish settlement in Delaware (1638—1655). Helsinki University Library / Matti Ruotsalainen.

feature of the Swedish society of estates of Early Modern Times. This did not exclude the presence of conflicts.[14]

In his book on rebellion in Finland, Kimmo Katajala underscores the point that both interaction and subjugation were integral parts of the mechanisms of society in Early Modern Times and they

---

[14]   Petri Karonen, *Pohjoinen suurvalta: Ruotsi ja Suomi 1521–1809* (Porvoo, 1999). Karonen rejects, with due cause, Tilly's above-mentioned view of Sweden as a state essentially based on coercion (pp. 329–331).

should not be regarded as mutually exclusive alternatives.[15] I came to this conclusion in my study on Finland during the period of the Great Northern War. The subjects influenced matters not only through forums approved and utilized by the crown but also in ways that the crown found undesirable and were criminalized by it.[16] According to Katajala, the strengthening of the crown's apparatus of control in the 17th century made it increasingly difficult for the peasants to carry out acts of mass violence or to threaten with such acts. They could resort to illegal means of pressure, i.e. rebel against the nobles at the level of the manors and estates, but the focus now shifted to political, administrative and judicial influence. The peasants used the *Riksdag* to repel the attempts of the crown to gain dominance and, with the aid of the other estates, also those of the nobility in the social political sphere.[17]

The question arises, however, whether the peasantry had other means than rebellion to take care of matters at the manor level.

Recent Swedish studies have largely rejected the traditional concept established by Eli F. Heckscher and others that the nobility

---

15 Kimmo Katajala, *Suomalainen kapina: Talonpoikaislevottomuudet ja poliittisen kulttuurin muutos Ruotsin ajalla (n. 1150–1800)* (Helsinki, 2002), p. 491.

16 Antti Kujala, *Miekka ei laske leikkiä: Suomi suuressa pohjan sodassa 1700–1714* (Helsinki, 2001), in particular pp. 335–343.

17 Since the reign of Gustavus II Adolphus (1611–1632), the consent of the *Riksdag* was required for issuing or amending laws and for decreeing new taxes or conscription. The *Riksdag*'s right of consent also extended to declaring war and agreeing to peace. It proved, however, that neither the government nor in particular the monarch upon reaching maturity age did not completely recognize nor follow this procedure, which was in force for the most part. For the peasants, the role of an estate of the *Riksdag* was not only a right but also a tedious and costly obligation. It was expensive to send representative and the peasants well understood that the system bound them to the decisions and rulings and made them pay for them. Four estates were represented at the *Riksdag*: the nobility, the clergy, the burghers and the peasants. Tax and crown peasants paying taxes to the crown as well as the donated-land tax peasants belonged to the estate of the peasantry and elected their representatives through indirect ballot and under the supervision of the authorities. Donated-land tenant farmers, i.e. old donated-land peasants and crown peasants assigned to donated land as well as the landless population remained outside the estate of the peasantry. See e.g. Katajala, *Suomalainen kapina*, pp. 285–291, 322–329.

threatened the freedom of the peasantry by systematically seeking to obtain the rights of inheritance of the peasants of their donated tax-yielding lands.[18] This correction is no doubt necessary, but the leniency of the nobility in their manors and estates has been slightly overemphasized. This is due to the practice common, though not predominant, practice in Swedish research of selecting individual examples, here one or a few members of the high nobility, of whom broader generalizations are made explicitly or implicitly.

DOMINATION AND EVERYDAY RESISTANCE

According to the American anthropologist James C. Scott, peasant rebellions and revolutions in particular are a rare phenomenon. Situations favourable to their outbreak occur only rarely and when a rebellion takes place it is quelled almost without exception. A defeated rebellion may sometimes lead to concessions and remissions, but this uncertain possibility carries little weight alongside the repression and demoralization that inevitably follow defeat.

For these reasons, Scott maintains the importance of focusing on the everyday forms of peasant resistance instead of rebellion, i.e. on the prosaic yet continuous struggle between the peasants and those trying to exact corvée or wage labour, land rent, interest or taxes from them. Most of this everyday opposition does not reach the level of collective opposition. Everyday resistance is a matter of "the weapons of the weak", such as foot dragging, dissimulation, false compliance, feigned ignorance, pilfering, slander, boycott, arson, sabotage and military desertion.

---

[18] Eli F. Heckscher, *Sveriges ekonomiska historia från Gustav Vasa*, I:2 (Stockholm, 1936), pp. 303–336; Kurt Ågren, *Adelns bönder och kronans: Skatter och besvär i Uppland 1650– 1680* (Uppsala, 1964), passim; Margareta Revera, *Gods och gård 1650–1680: Magnus Gabriel De la Gardies godsbildning och godsdrift i Västergötland*, I (Uppsala, 1975), passim; Eibert Ernby, *Adeln och bondejorden: En studie rörande skattefrälset i Oppunda härad under 1600-talet* (Uppsala, 1975), passim.

The benefit of everyday resistance is that it calls for only a little or hardly any coordination or planning, and avoids open clashes with the authority of the opposing side, which might have unfortunate consequences. Covert resistance will often have only marginal results, but owing to the hegemony of those in power, the peasants have no other recourse.

Scott discovered indications of "the weapons of the weak" by observing the life of a Malaysian village in the 1970s. Their arsenal of means was partly the same, but partly different, from that of Finnish peasants of the 17th and 18th centuries. The world observed and documented by Scott entailed solely or for the most part the most concealed forms of insubordination and opposition.[19] Everyday opposition can be recognized more often from related intent than from any practical consequences.

Scott also discusses the hegemony maintained by those who are in power in a community. This hegemony claims that the existing order is fair for all. He also refers to the level of public activity where the disenfranchised rarely challenge those in power in any direct manner. At this level everything follows the rules of official ideology and order. Through their obedient behaviour, the poor accept the relations of power and are able to enjoy the charity promised to them by the prevailing ideology. Protest takes place in discussions among the poor and in their thoughts (by no means least through mocking authority), and through the covert resistance discussed above. The incomplete realization of the ideals of official ideology does not remain unnoticed among the poor. They do not believe in this ideology in the form that it is offered to them, but instead they develop a version of it that corresponds to their own sense of justice.[20]

---

[19] On the concepts of insubordination, resistance and protest, see Kujala, *Miekka ei laske leikkiä*, pp. 18-25 and cited literature. See also Werner Rösener, *Peasants in the Middle Ages* (Cambridge, 1992), pp. 237–251.

[20] James C. Scott, *Weapons of the Weak: Everyday Forms of Peasant Resistance* (New Haven, 1975), pp. 28–41, 289–350 and passim.

Coat of arms of the Duchy of South-Finland. Etching and engraving in Erik Dahlberg's illustrated work *Suecia antiqua et hodierna*. National Board of Antiquities.

With regard to Finland in the 17th and 18th centuries, the experience of Malaysian peasants analysed by Scott 25 years ago appears to be more relevant than the experiences and reality of early modern European peasant and lower-class rebellions and tax-related revolts and riots[21]. He has obviously succeeded in discovering certain permanent features of human communal behaviour in conditions where the common people do not dare to openly resist authority.

Barrington Moore in turn maintains that all societies draw certain limits to what those in power and their subjects can do. A system of mutual obligations binds both groups together. These boundaries and obligations are not defined by any written constitution, and those in power and their subjects continuously test them in practice to see how much benefit they can gain and where permitted behaviour becomes insubordination. The parties are not equal, but the subjects nonetheless have recognized moral demands and requirements with regard to those in power.[22]

According to the interpretation of medieval conditions presented by the Austrian social historian Otto Brunner (1939) there was a mutually binding system of rights and obligations (*Herrschaft*) between the master (knight) and his vassal. The peasant had to pay his regular rent and assist his master with extraordinary taxes in addition to serving him. The master was required to protect his vassals. If he failed to do so, the peasant ceased to be under obligation to him, and could change masters or even rebel. Brunner notes that this was an unequal relationship where the

---

[21]   Yves-Marie Bercé, *Histoire des Croquants* (Paris, 1986); William Beik, *Urban Protest in Seventeenth-Century France: The Culture of Retribution* (Cambridge, 1997); Peter Blickle, *Unruhen in der ständischen Gesellschaft 1300–1800* (München, 1988); Blickle, *Der Bauernkrieg: Die Revolution des Gemeinen Mannes* (München, 1998). An example of a tax revolt of the kind that did not come about in Finland is given in: José Cubero, *Une révolte antifiscale au XVIIe siècle: Audijos soulève la Gascogne (1664–1675)* (Paris, 2001).

[22]   Barrington Moore Jr., *Injustice: The Social Bases of Obedience and Revolt* (London, 1978), especially pp. 3–48. E. P. Thompson's 1971 formulation of the 'moral economy of the crowd' means almost the same as Moore's recognized moral demands of the subjects. See E. P. Thompson, *Customs in Common* (Harmondsworth, 1993), pp. 185–258 (– 351).

master was nonetheless also dependent on the peasant.[23] Werner Rösener, a modern-day scholar of peasant history rejects Brunner's suggestion that mutual dependency would have often overcome conflicts and prevented them from eruption. Brunner's views, however, have to a considerable degree become the basis of the so-called Nordic interaction model. In fact, it seems obvious that all conceptions of the principle of reciprocity (or the moral economy of the crowd) that have also been expressed in one form or another even outside the Nordic countries derive from Brunner's writings, and if not from them then at least from studies on medieval vassal relations.[24]

Peter Reinholdsson has transferred Brunner's ideas of a system of reciprocal obligations between the landlord and the peasants to the Late Middle Ages in Sweden. But coming from the University of Uppsala, he does not use the concept of interaction, which is particularly popular among scholars at the University of Lund. According to Reinholdsson, the lending of seed grain and reductions of rent in times of crop failure were among the

---

[23] Otto Brunner, *Land und Herrschaft: Grundfragen der territorialen Verfassungsgeschichte Österreichs im Mittelalter*, 5. Aufl. (Darmstadt, 1990), pp. 254–303, 343–348. The reciprocity of the medieval vassal relationship was also underlined by Marc Bloch. Marc Bloch, *Feudal Society*, I (Chicago, 1993), pp. 227–230. According to Natalie Zemon Davis, the gift institute (gratitude) that she studied and alongside it contracts (the sale) and coercion maintained dependency between the sectors and individual members of society and accordingly the social system. Natalie Zemon Davis, *The Gift in Sixteenth-Century France* (Madison, 2000). According to the traditional Japanese view, the individual was in an eternal debt of gratitude to his feudal lord (and later to the Emperor), his parents and ancestors. This debt was repaid with respect, gifts and services, but it could never be sufficiently recompensed. A different, repayable relationship of debt bound (and still binds) more or less equal individuals. Services must be repaid to the opposite party to the letter. Ruth Benedict, *The Crysanthemum and the Sword* (Tokyo, 1954). No society can be maintained solely through coercion. It also needs the above-mentioned mutual dependency of its members and the acceptability (at least partial) of the system as factors maintaining it.

[24] Rösener, *Peasants in the Middle Ages*, pp. 237–238. Peter Burke suggests that E. P. Thompson's suggestion of the moral economy stems from the tradition established by the Hungarian scholar Karl Polanyi, who distinguished three forms of exchange for goods and services: reciprocity, redistribution and market exchange. Karl Polanyi, *The Great Transformation: The Political and Economic Origins of Our Time* (Boston, 1957); Peter Burke, *History and Social Theory* (Polity Press, 1998), pp. 69–71.

measures of protection accorded by the master to the vassal. At that time, holders of tax-exempt estates appeared to have been particularly dependent on the support of their peasants. The relationship of dependency included a strong ethical obligation. Both parties were expected to work for the common good and not only to pursue their own interests greedily. In serving the peasants satisfactorily, protection obtained the necessary legitimazion for the relationship of dependence; in other cases the landlords could look forward to considerable difficulties.[25]

In Norway, Sweden and Finland in the 17th century there was a relationship of interaction in many matters between those in power and their subjects, and peasant freedoms largely survived. According to Eva Österberg, interaction was not symmetrical, in other words the parties involved were not equal. As noted above, interaction has to be complemented with the theme of the power state insofar as, in principle, everything happened upon the terms of those who were in power. The concrete parameters and extent of interaction depended on the matter at hand, the forum in question and the prevailing situation in society.

According to Charles Tilly, those in power react to pressure with bargaining. This element is included even in repression: only the worst insurgents – instead of everyone – are punished. For those in power interaction means the binding of their subordinates to the system of exercising power by confirming their rights and prerogatives and by recognizing their influence. It is simply a question of a mechanism of power.[26] Accordingly, Jan Lindegren views the binding of Swedish peasants to the exercise of power as a system whereby the power state obtained a great deal of legitimacy, and using it to harness with exceptional efficiency the resources of society (taxation, conscription).[27]

---

[25] Peter Reinholdsson, *Uppror eller resningar?: Samhällsorganisation och konflikt i senmedeltidens Sverige* (Uppsala, 1998), pp. 146–219. Also Katajala, *Suomalainen kapina*, p. 202.

[26] Tilly, *Coercion, Capital, and European States*, pp. 99–103.

[27] Jan Lindegren, 'Ökade ekonomiska krav och offentliga bördor 1550–1750,' *Lokalsamfunn og øvrighet i Norden ca. 1550–1750*, H. Winge (ed.) (Oslo, 1992), pp. 201–202.

Commander in the wars against the imperial forces in Germany and against Poland and Denmark, Carl Gustav Wrangel (1613–1676) built Skokloster castle in Uppland between the 1650s and '70s. The stateliest manor house in the 17th century Sweden, the construction costs of the castle amounted to approximately the same sum as the contemporary annual expenditure of the Province of Åbo and Björneborg. Wrangel's income derived from his high offices as well as from the donated lands he possessed in various parts of the realm. As from the year 1651, he held the County of Salmis in the Province of Kexholm. Due to the military expeditions and plundering by the Russians in the Province of Kexholm in the 1650s, and to the insufficient return provided by the county, Wrangel gave up this donation – which had given him the rank of count – in 1665 (1669), exchanging it for the County of Sölvesborg in Blekinge.

Peter Englund has described the attitudes of the 17th-century nobility towards the peasants in terms of paternalism. The nobleman and the peasant were at the opposite ends of the spectrum of unequal class society, in which a relationship of mutual obligations existed. The love between them was expressed

29

in the fact that the nobleman commanded and the peasant obeyed and carried out his obligations. Englund maintains that a bare relationship of subjugation lay at the root of such love. The closeness and personal nature of the relationship was mostly the theatre of power, in which the daily role game ensured that everything remained unchanged. Also the ideology of society as a hierarchical organism in which each class or estate had the duties and rights belonging to its station supported the existing order. All attempts to disturb this state of affairs, declared to be harmonious, would only lead to disorder.

But it was the ideal of the nobility to treat their peasants well and this ideal was often realized in practice. Englund underlines the point that also the peasants could influence the rules of the game of power, and use them to their own advantage. One of the most efficient means was to appeal to the benevolence of those who were in power. Moreover, most members of the nobility understood well that it would be politically short-sighted to place too great a strain on the peasants. This would endanger the legitimacy of power and might lead to rebellion.[28]

Stephen Vlastos has described the attitudes of 17th-century Japanese feudal lords to their peasants as the political economy of benevolence. This meant that in the long term it was wiser to ease the taxation of the peasants than to lead them to ruin through inflexibility, thus losing their tax revenue and even leading them to insubordination.[29] The Swedish state followed precisely the

---

[28] Peter Englund, *Det hotade huset: Adliga föreställningar om samhället under stormaktstiden* (Stockholm, 1994), especially pp. 25–48, 90–102, 194–204. On the hierachical model of a society of the estates involving prayer, combat and production, see also Georges Duby, *The Three Orders: Feudal Society Imagined* (Chicago, 1980). On petitions, see *Petitions in Social History*, Lex Heerma van Voss (ed.), International Review of Social History, Supplement 9 (Cambridge, 2001).

[29] Stephen Vlastos, *Peasant Protests and Uprisings in Tokugawa Japan* (Berkeley, 1990), pp. 15–17, 34–41, 44. David Moon observed that also the land-owning and ruling elite of Russia felt it was their obligation to protect the peasants against undue exploitation, i.e. the system of mutual obligations also prevailed here. The peasants, in turn, utilized the ideal of good master and required their superiors to behave accordingly. David Moon, *The Russian Peasantry 1600–1930* (London, 1999), pp. 88–89, 272–273.

same policy in granting tax exemptions and reductions to peasants in times of crop failure.

It can be asked how the state in general could have ruled without the organs of local self-government as its resources were in any case much smaller than in the 19th or 20th centuries.

In my earlier studies I have applied the above concept of interaction and the system of mutual obligations to taxation, viewing it as a kind of social contract, a compromise between the rights of the crown and the obligations of the estates and the subjects. The fact that as much as possible was defined in fixed quantities usually corresponded to the interests of the subjects and was a concession towards them. For the crown, this meant the predictability and planned nature of managing the economy. The monarch could agree to this system, because its rules permitted him to increase the obligations of his subjects on the grounds of some unexpected need such as war. Until the 1680s and 1690s the king required the approval of the *Riksdag* for extraordinary auxiliary taxes and levies, but since the emergence of autocracy he was capable of levying contributions without convening the estates. The cadastre, with its fixed amounts of taxes laid down for all farming properties was thus a social contract and extraordinary auxiliary taxes, contributions and other payments were the crown's means of bypassing it. Taxes that were too high yet fixed were a better alternative for the peasant than giving the crown completely free rein to raise taxes.[30]

Åsa Karlsson has demonstrated that as late as 1713 the peasants of Uppland in Middle Sweden still subscribed to the medieval reciprocal concept whereby the peasants were entitled to demand defence and protection from the crown in return for the payment of taxes.[31]

---

[30]   Kujala, *Miekka ei laske leikkiä*, p. 75; Kujala, 'Why Did Finland's War Economy Collapse during the Great Northern War?,' *Scandinavian Economic History Review* 2001, p. 85.

[31]   Åsa Karlsson, *Den jämlike undersåten: Karl XII:s förmögenhetsskatt 1713* (Uppsala, 1994), pp. 222–224. On reciprocity, see also Torkel Jansson, *Agrarsamhällets förändring och landskommunal organisation: En konturteckning av 1800-talets Norden* (Uppsala, 1987), p. 18.

The Wrangels were originally a noble German family from the Baltic provinces. Carl Gustav had studied at the University of Leiden. He was interested in culture but had a passion for warfare and bounties. It is precisely the commanders like Wrangel that made Sweden into a great power. As the governor-general of Pomerania, Wrangel was close to new potential war fronts. Towards the end of 1674, the then ageing and gouty military commander led the Swedish troops, short of provisions, to Brandenburg to be maintained and fed there. The subsidies paid by France to Sweden as well as the bribes silently paid to the regency members Wrangel and M.G. De la Gardie got Sweden once again involved in a wider European conflict. However, in the battle of Fehrbellin in 1675, Brandenburg defeated the Swedes. It became obvious to everybody that the Swedish army was no longer what it used to be. Denmark and some other countries lost no time to declare war to be able to divide the bounty. Oil on canvas by Matthaeus Merian, the 17th century. National Board of Antiquities.

The present volume studies whether this reciprocity also applied in relations between the nobility and their tenants, and where its boundaries lay in 17th-century society. In slightly simplified terms the borders of reciprocity mean to what degree the actions and behaviour of people were defined by this principle and to what degree by rational interests defined in "pure terms" independent of ideological and mental structures.

The present study thus investigates the correctness of the concepts of the power state and interaction model in 17th and early 18th-century Sweden and Finland with reference to crown taxation and manorial economy. I seek to establish how and with what degree of success the peasants attended to their interests at the basic and lower levels of 17th and early 18th century.[32] The study is based on conditions in Finland and in particular in Southwestern Finland, consisting of the provinces of Åbo and Björneborg and Nyland and Tavastehus. Since the provinces of Finland did not enjoy any special status in the 17th century among in the core areas of the Swedish realm consisting of Sweden and Finland[33] and because West-Finnish society was in other respects largely similar to Swedish society, the results are also relevant with regard to Sweden. In the late 17th century, when the provinces conquered from Denmark were incorporated in the Swedish realm, Finland became a minor and peripheral part of the realm. Despite this, it was a far larger entity than that the individual district, parish or nobleman that has often been the focus in Swedish historical research. Therefore the results of the

---

[32] The political influence of the upper levels of the peasantry via the *Riksdag* is thoroughly investigated in Katajala's book *Suomalainen kapina*, and it is unnecessary to repeat the same points here.

[33] Sweden and Finland formed the core area of the realm, around which conquered territories in the Baltics (Estonia and Livonia) as well as Ingermanland and the Province of Kexholm (which is not discussed at all in the present study) and territories in Germany were later assembled. Unlike the other new conquests, the provinces annexed from Denmark were soon integrated into the core areas of the realm, i.e. Sweden. On the conglomerate nature of the Swedish realm, see Harald Gustafsson, 'The Conglomerate State: A Perspective on State Formation in Early Modern Europe,' *Scandinavian Journal of History* 1999, pp. 189–213.

research are relevant for both Finland and Sweden. (Hopefully they are relevant also in a wider European context.)

THE SYSTEM OF TAXATION

The crown's system of taxation[34] had come about during the course of several centuries as new taxes accumulated alongside the former ones. The system was complex with considerable local differences. The majority of taxes in Finland and in Sweden in general were collected from the peasantry, the largest class in society.[35] The core of the land rent paid by the peasants consisted of the cadastral or annual rent (*jordeboksräntan / årliga räntan*). Each holding (farm) paid this tax on the basis of its solvency and the corresponding taxation units that were in use in the district and province in question in accordance with the size of the tax marked for the holding in the provincial cadastre (*jordebok*). The annual rent (as also the so-called military expedition tax) was mainly laid down in the form of produce (tax items) and only to lesser degree in cash. The prices of products were converted into money according to crown values that were lower than the market prices. Linking the taxes to products protected the receiving party of the taxes against the deterioration of the value of money. The annual rent was the largest individual tax in terms of both burden and yield.

---

[34] A basic work on the history of taxation and tax systems is Gabriel Ardent, *Histoire de l'impôt*, I–II (Fayard, 1971–1972). Also Ardent, 'Financial Policy and Economic Infrastructure of Modern States and Nations,' *The Formation of National States in Western Europe*, Charles Tilly (ed.) (Princeton, 1975), pp. 164–242.

[35] There were naturally differences in wealth and affluence among the peasants. Beneath the peasantry there was still the landless population, from among which the crown recruited most of its troops, with the assistance of the peasant community. The most repressive features of society were implemented in relation to the landless population. On the landless population, see Eino Jutikkala, 'Väestö ja yhteiskunta,' *Hämeen historia*, II:1 (Hämeenlinna, 1957), pp. 188–209, 381 and passim.

Gustav Vasa (reigned 1523–1560) had decreed for the crown two-thirds of the church tithes, the so-called crown tithes. The remaining one third went to the clergy. The *lagman* and district justice taxes were used to fund their salaries.

Uncertain taxes (*ovissa räntor*) had been converted into permanent taxes. The uncertain taxes were laid down for each homestead (*hemman*) according to its designation (*hemmantal*) or assessment unit (*mantal*). The homestead was a cameral concept which did not always correspond to a real holding or farm, since the designations had remained listed unchanged in the cadastre, which did not recognize the splitting or joining of holdings subsequent to their initial listing. The assessment unit *mantal* (or *gärdemantal*, auxiliary tax unit) was an arithmetic figure, which (like the older province- or district-based tax unit which was the basis for assessing the annual rent) was meant to express the yield and tax-paying ability of the holding or farm. The military expedition tax defined according to the assessment unit *mantal* was the second-largest individual tax after the annual rent and the most important so-called uncertain tax. The other uncertain taxes were on a cash basis.

Extraordinary taxes (*extra ordinarie räntor*) were the youngest stratum of the regular taxes. They were made permanent around the middle of the 17th century. Extraordinary taxes (livestock fees, transport fees, auxiliary day-labour fees etc.) were paid according to the *mantal* assessment unit or in some cases according to the designation, and they were on a cash basis. The crown also calculated the poll-tax as extraordinary tax. With considerable exceptions the poll-tax was paid by all adult persons.

Alongside the taxes that had been made permanent the crown also collected temporary auxiliary taxes or contributions. The *Riksdag* agreed to their being levied for specific purposes for set periods of time. In 1693 the *Riksdag* waived this right for the duration of the war. The diet had already lost its peace-time right to influence taxation somewhat earlier. These changes were associated with the emergence of autocracy. The contributions were paid also on other bases than landed property, and even the other estates, including the nobility, had to pay their share.

The inhabitants of the towns and cities paid partly the same taxes as the rural population, for example the poll-tax. Urban-dwellers also had their own crown taxes (and municipal taxes) to pay. The crown also levied indirect crown taxes in the towns: large maritime duties applied to foreign trade and the so-called small duty was levied on all foodstuffs and consumer goods that were brought into the towns.[36] In the 1620s and 1630s crown taxation was increased to fund wars[37] to such a high level that it was hardly possible to raise it any more. At the time, the annual rent and taxes consumed all the yield of land in use by the peasantry. After the 1640s the tax burden hardly increased any more and in good years a surplus remained from the farms after payment of tax,[38] especially since the arable areas of the farms was gradually increasing towards the close of the century. In most parts of Finland, the peasants had only taken under recultivation the fields that had become overgrown with grass and forest in the late 16th and early 17th century. Farming did not progress beyond that extent.[39]

Field areas and amounts of sown grain per household and capita in the various historical provinces of Finland have been assessed from the sowing tax lists of the 1620s and 1630s and also from surveyors' maps. Arable area per farm (and also per capita with regard to the extended families of Karelia) diminished from west to east, from south to north, although Tavastia and Satakunta (at least Lower Satakunta on the coast) competed on

---

[36]   Jutikkala, *Bonden i Finland genom tiderna* (a basic work on the Finnish peasantry and taxation).

[37]   Against Poland 1621–1629; in 1630, Sweden entered the Thirty Years' War (1618–1648).

[38]   Jutikkala, 'Väestö ja yhteiskunta,' pp. 142–144; Lindegren, 'Ökade ekonomiska krav och offentliga bördor,' p. 192; Pentti Virrankoski, 'Pohjois-Pohjanmaa ja Lappi 1600-luvulla,' *Pohjois-Pohjanmaan ja Lapin historia,* III (Oulu, 1973), pp. 465–466; Eero Matinolli, 'Kruunun-verotus,' *Varsinais-Suomen historia,* VI:4 (Turku, 1976), pp. 48, 50.

[39]   Eino Jutikkala, 'Suurien sotien ja uuden asutusekspansion kaudet,' *Suomen taloushistoria,* I (Helsinki, 1980), pp. 171–177.

The Kingdom of Sweden and the historical provinces of Sweden and Finland
1660–1700

an equal footing with Finland-Proper. The amounts of sown grain reveal similar proportions among the provinces. Property in livestock among the provinces, which can also be estimated on the part of the 1620s and 1630s, decreased from west to east, and in Southern Finland from the coast towards the inland. Livestock ownership in the Åland Islands and Southern Ostrobothnia even exceeded the figures for Southwest Finland in terms of head of cattle per farm.[40]

There are no similar lists of sown-grain or livestock tax for the second half of the 17th century, and at least in the Province of Åbo and Björneborg – with the exception of the Åland Islands – each farm paid in the 1670s and 1690s always the same amount of tithes assigned to it, with the total amount of tithes varying by parish and county only according to how many farms at the time had been classed as unable to pay tax.[41] As the amounts of tithes had been fixed, they cannot be used for deducing annual amounts of sown grain (good and bad years) any more than possible trends of affluence.

According to the instructions for the new levying of taxes that came into use in the 1690s in many Swedish provinces as also in the provinces of Nyland and Tavastehus and Åbo and Björneborg, half of the yield of the farm belonged to the crown and half to the farmer after the subtraction of sown grain (and tithes). This, however, was only a norm that was followed when reassessing the taxation of farms, and the overall situation on the farms was more complex, with exceptions in both directions.[42]

A permanent risk factor for agriculture was provided by late spring seasons, night frosts in the autumn, aridity and exceptional

---

[40]   Jutikkala op.cit., pp. 171–177, 193–197, 214–218; Armas Luukko, *Suomen historia 1617–1721* (Porvoo, 1967), pp. 128–144.

[41]   Seppo Muroma, *Suurten kuolovuosien (1696–1697) väestönmenetys Suomessa* (Helsinki, 1991), pp. 15–16. I have checked the same point with regard to the early 1670s in the mainland parts of the Province of Åbo and Björneborg..

[42]   Riksarkivet (RA), Stockholm, Kammararkivet, Kamreraren D. Norbergs kontor, F III:1, Skattläggningsmetoderna i Sverige och Finland, 1690-talet (Kansallisarkisto [KA], Helsinki, microfilm FR 647); Matinolli, 'Kruununverotus,' pp. 19–24.

rainfall, which would use up the surplus of the farms and could lead to famine. The so-called minor ice age was at its worst in the 17th century, when at least every third year was marked by crop failure. Every second year was either poor or one of crop failure.[43] According to variation in the price of rye, the years 1662–1664, 1675–1677, 1682 and 1694–1699 were the worst occasions of crop failure.[44]

In principle, unpaid taxes for a period of three years would make the peasant lose his so-called hereditary rights (*bördsrätt*) to his farm. Not only the so-called abandonment of a holding, i.e. its official inability to pay taxes but also temporary exemption from taxes or reduced taxation (*förmedling*) would in many cases lead to the loss of family or hereditary rights. Unlike in the case of the hereditary or tax peasant (*skattebonde*), the crown did not even recognize usufruct for a crown peasant (*kronobonde*) who had lost his family rights. Consequently, the crown or a nobleman could freely evict such a peasant if they felt that changing the farmer could ensure better management and payment of taxes for the farm.

In principle, the nobility levied from their peasants on donated or enfeoffed land (*frälsebönder*) everything that the crown had demanded, i.e. all the taxes and labour service which the crown had relinquished now came to benefit the recipient of the donation. If the donated-land peasants were crown peasants, i.e. having lost their hereditary rights, they were in the same position regarding tax paid to their landlord as the so-called old donated-land peasants (*gamla frälsebönder*) on properties that had already for a longer time been in the ownership of the nobility. The term for tax-

---

[43]   K. R. & G. Melander, 'Katovuosista Suomessa,' *Oma Maa,* V (Porvoo, 1924), pp. 353–359; Virrankoski, 'Pohjois-Pohjanmaa ja Lappi 1600-luvulla,' pp. 205–213; Matleena Tornberg, 'Ilmaston- ja sadonvaihtelut Lounais-Suomessa 1550-luvulta 1860-luvulle,' *Turun historiallinen arkisto* 44 1989, pp. 58–71; Jutikkala, 'Suurien sotien ja uuden asutusekspansion kaudet,' pp. 197–202.

[44]   Johan Adolf Lindström, 'Kumo Socken uti historiskt hänseende,' *Suomi,* XX (1860), pp. 296–297.

Venngarn castle in Uppland, mid-17th century, built by the Chancellor of the Realm Magnus Gabriel De la Gardie (1622–1686), one of the favourites of Queen Christina (prior to falling into her disgrace) and a member of the regency during King Charles XI's infancy (1660–1672). De la Gardie failed as a military commander under Charles X Gustav and Charles XI, and neither was he a particularly firm decision-maker when serving in government. His lack of determined direction was hidden by his eloquence. De la Gardie was one of the most prosperous men in the realm until Charles XI destroyed his economic and political powers and status during restitution and the process against the regency. De la Gardie's annual expenses in 1679 were slightly in excess of the combined annual expenditure of the provinces of Åbo and Björneborg and Nyland and Tavastehus in 1680. De la Gardie made property arrangements to leave it to his heirs and to save the holdings from restitution – in vain, as it turned out later. He was a great patron of arts and treated his peasants fairly well. From Erik Dahlberg's illustrated work *Suecia antiqua et hodierna*. National Board of Antiquities.

exempt land (*frälsejord*) originally meant land exempted from crown tax that members of the nobility could own in lieu of mounted service provided by them for the crown. Only the nobility were entitled to own such land. (Leading official positions were reserved for the nobility, and noble degrees were hereditary.

The monarch could raise to the nobility subjects who had performed important services for him and the realm.)

The old donated-land peasants and former crown peasants who been donated with tax-free land were tenant farmers (*landbor*) who paid their landlords rent on a private or contractual basis. The size and nature of the rent were defined by the landlord, at least in theory in agreement with the tenant, and were not bound by the payments of tax entered into the crown cadastre. In practice, it was often impossible to raise the crown taxes from their previous level, because the tenant would not have been able to pay, but the composition of the tax paid by peasants without hereditary rights could be changed by altering the proportion of day labour (whereby the tax burden would be reduced nominally but not in real terms – day labour was a considerable encumbrance for the peasant's management of his own farm, auxiliary means of livelihood and his freedom). On the other hand, the peasants who had preserved their hereditary rights paid their cadastrally listed taxes to their nobleman landlord and their day-labour services in 1651–1652 were given a maximum definition (18 auxiliary labour days per year for a whole farm unless the landlord and the peasants had agreed otherwise by mutual contract; a peasant living over two Swedish miles (21 kilometres) from the manor was permitted to perform his day-labour services in the form of a cash payment).[45]

---

[45]   Ågren & Revera, above-mentioned works, passim; Nilsson, *De stora krigens tid*, pp. 31–55; Jutikkala, *Bonden i Finland genom tiderna*, pp. 149–176 and passim; A. A. Stiernman (ed.), *Alla Riksdagars och Mötens Besluth, II, 1633–1680* (Stockholm, 1729), pp. 1194–1195 (1166–1167); KA, Kungliga plakater och förordningar, 26.8.1651. In addition to auxiliary or extraordinary day-labour services decreed by the *Riksdag* or the monarch we must take into account that the annual rent included a small number of labour days that could be paid in ready money to the crown, but not so in most cases to the nobles. When the peasant tenant farmer was cultivating the nobleman's manor land or the land of a non-noble member of the upper classes on contractual rent, he was in a slightly different position than the above-mentioned tenants of the nobles. Manors or their nearby properties could be given to be farmed by a tenant or tenants on the basis of a sharecropping agreement (Sw. *hälftenbruk*, Fr. *métayage*) whereby the crop was divided in two among the manor owner and the tenant after deduction of seed and taxes. The latter were also paid on a shared basis by both parties. Instead of this

Table 1. Payments and services to the crown from peasants on donated land in relation to peasants providing tax revenue for the crown after 1644

	Säter estate or boundary homesteads	Within freedom mile	Other
1. Annual rent	0	0	0
2. Uncertain taxes	0	0	0
3. Extraordinary	0	0	1/2
4. Justice taxes	0	1	1
5. Tithes	0	1	1
6. Conscription	0	0	1/2

Source: Ågren, *Adelns bönder och kronans*, p. 13 (1 = the same encumbrance as for peasants providing tax revenue for the crown)

A nobleman could establish a *säter* estate on one or several of his holdings by requesting permission for doing so from the king or the local governor – in practice this often only required notification

---

arrangement, the nobles could farm their manors themselves or lease them (or parts thereof) to an upper-class person to be farmed. Eino Jutikkala, *Läntisen Suomen kartanolaitos Ruotsin vallan viimeisenä aikana*, I (Helsinki, 1932), p. 131 ff (volumes I–II of Jutikkala's work discuss the manor system of the 18th century, which in many respects was similar to that of the 17th century, albeit with differences; KA, judicial district of Vemo and Lower Satakunta I, judgment book 1681, p. 601, judicial district of Lower Satakunta II, judgment book 1682, pp. 143, 213, 1683, p. 299, judicial district of Masku and Vemo, judgment book 1987, p. 32, 1688, pp. 52, 119, judicial district of Lower Satakunta II, judgment book 1688, p. 324, 1690, p. 417, judicial district of Vemo and Lower Satakunta II, judgment book 1693, p. 409. On the Danish estate system, see *Det danske godssystem – udvikling och afvikling 1500–1919*, Carsten Porskrug Rasmussen et al. (eds) (Århus, 1987); Porskrug Rasmussen, 'Godssystemer i Sønderjylland fra 1500- til 1700-tallet,' *Bol og By* 1996, pp. 38–61. On the French system of *métayage*, see Pierre Goubert, *Les paysans français au XVIIe siècle* (Hachette, 1994), pp. 45–47. There is no suitable English equivalent to convey the meaning of *frälse* (or *gammalt frälse*).

of such intent to the authorities. In comparison with other tax-donated land the *säter* estate provided greater tax exemption also for the boundary peasant homesteads within the same village (*rå och rörshemman*) as the residence of the nobleman-landlord and for peasant holdings within the so-called freedom mile (*frihetsmilshemman*). *Säter* estates were partly established only to minimize taxes. Only part of them were converted into farming unity, and even those were cultivated with small-scale agricultural methods. For example, in comparison with the arable areas of the Danish *säter* estates, only few of their Finnish counterparts could be called large farms. The *säter* estate rights included the obligation to erect a manor building and to maintain it.[46]

The 17th-century accounts of Finland's donated estates have survived only in places and in fragmentary condition.[47] It is impossible to establish with any certainty whether the authority of the crown or that of the nobility was more difficult to bear. This is due not only to the paucity of accounts kept by the nobility but also to the fact that day-labour and other services were recorded imperfectly or not at all, and that neither these encumbrances nor conscription could easily be measured in money. The donated-land peasants of the nobles provided in relative terms half the number of soldiers for the service of the crown as those bound to the crown (*kronans behållna bönder*), while the *säter* estates and their immediate surroundings were

46   Eljas Orrman, 'Säteribildningen i Finland under 1600-talet,' *Kustbygd och centralmakt 1560–1721* (Helsingfors, 1987), pp. 277–294; Jutikkala, 'Suurten sotien ja uuden asutus-ekspansion kaudet,' p. 180. On the land-owning conditions of the nobles and crown in the Nordic countries at the beginning of Modern Times, see Eino Jutikkala, *Bonden – adelsmannen – kronan: Godspolitik och jordegendomsförhållanden i Norden 1550–1750* (København, 1979).
47   The present study mainly deals with noble estates in Southwestern Finland from which accounts have survived. The material is in the National Archives (Riksarkivet) of Sweden. The collections of the University of Lund (Sweden) have partly been studied, but parts (Artsjö and Jackarby manors) were bypassed. I have also used the limited 17th-century manorial archive collections of the Finnish National Archives (Kansallisarkisto) with accounting material. For reasons of available time, I have not investigated the noble estates of Northern and Southeastern Finland.

completely exempted from conscription. On the other hand, the donated-land peasants often had to relinquish their benefits in times of war.[48] The peasants on donated lands were required to recompense their landlords for alleviated military encumbrances through additional rent or day-labour services.

It should be noted that the tax and crown peasants were either bound to the crown (i.e. paying their taxes to it) or given over to the nobility, whereby the former were tax peasants on donated lands (*skattefrälsebönder*) and the latter were tenants, farmers on donated land without hereditary rights. The old donated-land peasants of the nobility were the other main group among the tenant farmers on donated land. The crown did not even in theory include the old donated estates of the nobility in its domain in other way than by decreeing a tax-assessment unit (*mantal*) for them and by listing the appropriate uncertain and extraordinary taxes. On the other hand, the crown still kept records of new donated estates received by the nobility as donations, through purchase or as security by listing their annual, uncertain and extraordinary taxes to the amount that it had originally levied them. The old donated land was thus fundamentally exempted from annual rent, and all other tax exemptions awarded to donated land were laid down separately. Unlike the old donated estates, the new donated land was still referred to in the cadastres as tax or crown holdings (homesteads of either tax or crown peasants) in accordance with their original nature. In other words, these holdings still belonged in theory to the domain of the crown. The old donated lands were completely in the ownership of the nobility and the inheritance of this property was not regulated by any restrictions. The new donations too were hereditary. On the other hand, except for allodial (new) donations – which were few and in fact unlawful – the crown regulated the inheritance of new donations in such a manner that for example holdings in

---

[48]   Hakon Swenne, *Svenska adelns ekonomiska privilegier 1612–1651* (Göteborg, 1933), p. 321; also Villstrand, *Anpassning eller protest*, passim.

The administrative provinces, judicial districts and towns of Finland
(including the Province of Kexholm) 1699

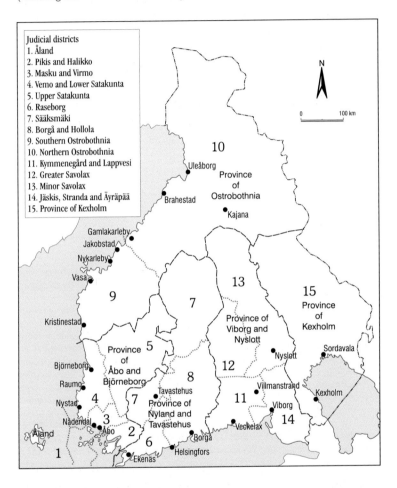

Judicial districts
1. Åland
2. Pikis and Halikko
3. Masku and Virmo
4. Vemo and Lower Satakunta
5. Upper Satakunta
6. Raseborg
7. Sääksmäki
8. Borgå and Hollola
9. Southern Ostrobothnia
10. Northern Ostrobothnia
11. Kymmenegård and Lappvesi
12. Greater Savolax
13. Minor Savolax
14. Jäskis, Stranda and Äyräpää
15. Province of Kexholm

accordance with the Norrköping resolution could only be inherited in direct succession in the male line. If there were no such descendants the holdings reverted to the crown.[49]

The Swedish peasant was not bound to the soil. He was free to move as long as he was not in arrears to his landlord, in which case he had to remain on the farm until he had cleared his debts. According to Eino Jutikkala, these situations were not very far removed from serfdom.[50]

---

[49] In principle, allodial, or eternal, donations given with unlimited rights of heritage were illegal, as the law forbade the king from reducing the crown revenue of his successors. The properties laid down according to the Norrköping *Riksdag* resolution of 1604 were the most common form of donation. The counties and baronies (*grev- och friherreskap*) were inherited undivided by the eldest son, and they included local administrative and judicial authority. The crown also forwarded tax revenue by selling and pledging properties, which were also hereditary. They could be redeemed at any time by the crown, but in practice there were no funds for this purpose. In addition to the inherited donations, there were still some enfeoffments that had been awarded indefinitely or for life. The old donated holdings had been obtained by the nobles before 1604 and unlike the new donations they were listed as *frälse* in the cadastres. The nobles were still able to transfer some properties into this category in the period from 1604 to 1632. The feudal doctrine of the shared right of land ownership did not become formulated in Sweden until the early 18th century, but in practice it was already followed in the 17th century. According to this doctrine, a peasant could at most have *dominium utile* or right of use (the right to inhabit and cultivate the property) – this applied to the tax peasants enjoying hereditary rights but not the crown peasants who had forfeited these rights or the tenant farmers. Ownership proper, *dominium directum*, provided the right to the yield of the land. If the peasant did not have hereditary rights, the crown or nobleman under whose authority he was had both *dominium directum* and *dominium utile*, i.e. complete right of ownership or *dominium plenum*. For the tax peasant, there was divided ownership, or *dominium divisum*, in both cases. Jutikkala, *Bonden i Finland genom tiderna*, pp. 149–166; Birger Ekeberg, *Om frälseränta: En rättshistorisk utredning* (Stockholm, 1911), pp. 10–11; Revera, *Gods och gård 1650–1680*, pp. 14, 86–87 and passim.

[50] Jutikkala, *Bonden i Finland genom tiderna*, pp. 173–174.

THE TAXATIONAL BASIS OF THE PROVINCES
OF FINLAND BEFORE AND
AFTER THE RESTITUTION OF DONATIONS

Table 2. Donated, enfeoffed, sold and pledged taxes in silver dalers in the four provinces of Finland

	Åbo-Björne-borg	Nyland-Tavaste-hus	Viborg	Ostro-bothnia
1653	117889	77430	71800	55843
1655	121851	77402	74054	
1670	114353	74615	56300	53839
1695	16510	21364	5970	2612

Sources: KA, 7250, 7257, 7313, 7399, 7956, 7961, 8001, 8071, 8610, 8616, 8667, 8714, 9137, 9155, 9209. The general ledgers of 1655 and 1670 for the Province of Ostrobothnia have not survived, and the figures for 1670 are taken from the year 1669. The 1670 ledger of the Province of Viborg has also been lost, and its data is replaced by the material for 1671. For the same reasons, the figures for 1694 are used for the Province of Nyland and Tavastehus.[51]

The above figures show that in 1670 the amount of tax revenue obtained by the nobility as a result of tax donations was at almost the same level as before the so-called one-quarter restitution decreed in 1655, which the nobility in most cases managed by paying the so-called quarter tax (a quarter of the taxes donated after 1632, and it was quite easy to be exempted even from

---

[51] This includes all the taxes within the sphere of the donations, including the so-called old donations, but not tax exemptions provided by the *säter* rights and the boundary rule and other measures. Nor has it been taken into account that at times donated lands paid contributions and the so-called quarter tax after the one-quarter restitution of 1655. For example in the Province of Åbo and Björneborg the quarter tax produced 13,647 dalers in 1670 (after subtraction of the 3,206 dalers of the restituted properties), but exemptions to the amount of 4,829 dalers were granted from it. KA, 7313.

Diagram 1. The structure of the main calculation of the crown accounts

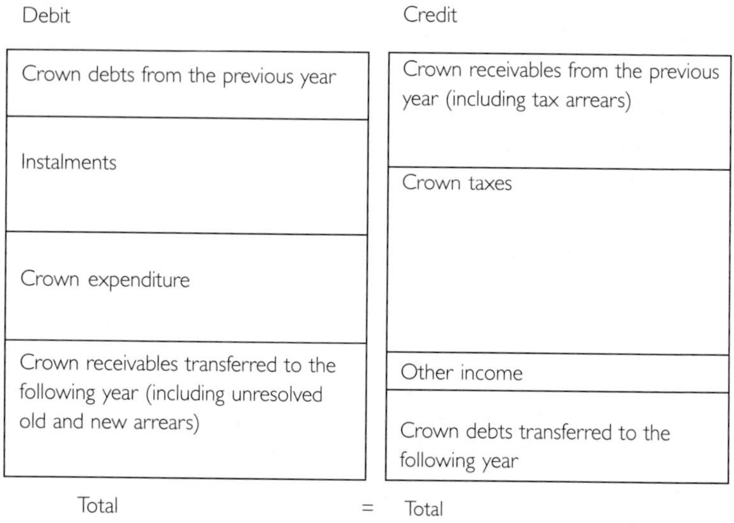

Debit		Credit	
Crown debts from the previous year		Crown receivables from the previous year (including tax arrears)	
Instalments		Crown taxes	
Crown expenditure			
Crown receivables transferred to the following year (including unresolved old and new arrears)		Other income	
		Crown debts transferred to the following year	
Total	=	Total	

If there were no major changes in the crown debts and receivables during the year, the sums of the instalments and crown expenditure of the debit column on the one hand and the crown taxes and other income of the credit column on the other hand should be approximately equal.

---

this).[52] The Province of Viborg was an exception to the almost unchanged tax donations. In this region donated land ceased to be attractive as a result of the attacks of the Russians into Eastern Savolax and the neighbouring regions of Ingermanland and the

---

[52] On the one-quarter restitution, see Stellan Dahlgren, *Karl X Gustav och reduktionen* (Uppsala, 1964), which concerned only donations granted after the year 1632. Allodial rights granted after the year 1632 were revoked.

Province of Kexholm during the war of 1656–1660.[53] These changes presumably also reflected the explicit aim of the crown to improve the economy of the armed forces in the Province of Viborg.

In 1670 in the Province of Åbo and Björneborg – with the exception of the Åland Islands which did not belong to the provincial financial administration – all crown instalments[54] (*avkortningarna*), i.e. tax that remained unreceived as the result of officially confirmed exemption totalled 187,408 and funds used by the crown (annual crown expenditure – *anordningarna*) amounted to 127,052 dalers. During this year in the Province of Nyland and Tavastehus, instalments amounted to 114,471 dalers and crown expenditure to 82,706 dalers. The corresponding figures were instalments of 87,982 and expenditure of 167,490 dalers in the Province of Viborg in 1671, and 75,718 / 33,954 dalers in the Province of Ostrobothnia in 1669. In the provinces of Åbo and Björneborg and Nyland and Tavastehus, the crown had thus donated to the nobility an amount of tax revenue almost equal to the taxes available to and used by the provincial economy.[55] If the crown had had possession of the taxes donated to the nobility, the funds used by the provincial financial administration would have almost doubled.

A more or less similar situation prevailed in almost all the provinces of Sweden proper, with the exception of Norrland in the north. In practice, however, the crown had donated

---

53 Jussi T. Lappalainen, *Kaarle X Kustaan Venäjän-sota v. 1656–1658 Suomen suunnalla* (Jyväskylä, 1972).

54 There were two main types of instalments: tax exemption granted on the basis of class privileges (tax donation) and the inability to pay taxes of the peasants

55 In both provinces the crown had to some degree other revenue than taxes alone. In the administrative district of Vemo almost all the *mantal* units (92%) were donations in 1670, and in the districts of Masku (74%), Pikis (63%) and Lower Satakunta (74%) they were a definite majority. In the upper (54%) and lower (52%) administrative districts of Upper Satakunta the donated *mantal* units were in a slight majority in relation to *mantals* witheld for the crown, but most of the *mantal* units (60%) in the district of Halikko were withheld for the crown in 1670. (The figures for Kimito Parish, however, are lacking on the part of the *mantal* units of the district of Halikko).

considerably less than half of its revenue to the nobility, because it had other major sources of income than taxes, above all customs duties. Owing to the concentration of foreign trade in Stockholm, the customs revenue was collected almost completely outside Finland. In the Province of Åbo and Björneborg customs revenue in 1670 amounted to only 12,592 silver dalers – 1% of the total figure for Finland and Sweden (conquered territories and also Skåne, Halland and Blekinge excepted). In 1670 the total volume of the Åbo and Björneborg provincial economy (funds used by the crown) was 2.7% of the economy of the whole realm (Sweden, Finland and conquered territories), in other words considerably more than its proportion of customs revenue. Calculated in similar terms, the volume of the economy of the four provinces of Finland in the early 1670s was 8.9% of the volume of the economy of the whole realm, a modest figure. The economy of the Finnish provinces can also be compared with economy of the whole realm with regard to taxes including instalments, and other revenue, in which case their proportion is 13.0%. Because the income of the Finnish provinces consisted to a greater degree of tax than other items and considerable instalments (taxes unpaid with due permission) were made to the tax revenue, the first-mentioned figure of 8.9% is a more accurate indication of the proportion of the Finnish provinces in the overall economy of the realm.[56] Belonging to the conquered territories and administratively adjacent to Ingermanland, the Province of Kexholm was not included among the provinces of Finland at the time.

According to the debit column of the main calculation of the 1669 general ledger of the realm, crown instalments amounted to 2,076,721 silver dalers, and funds used by the state to 4,634,857 dalers. Of all the tax instalments, those related to tax donations to the nobility totalled 1,371,631 dalers. At the level of the realm as a whole, the tax exemptions donated to the nobility were

---

56   KA, general ledgers of the provinces 1670 (1669–1671). In Sweden and Finland import duties produced an undeduced yield (i.e. including instalments) totalling 1,274,260 dalers. On the economy of the realm, see the following note.

approximately 30% of crown funds, which was considerably less than in the provinces of Southwest Finland. According to the credit column of the main calculation, all customs and mining revenue of the crown (only in Sweden and Finland) totalled 1,668,155 dalers, and all income (including customs and mining revenue) including instalments in Sweden and Finland amounted to 4,661,719 dalers. The corresponding figure for the realm as a whole, including the conquered territories — the former Danish provinces in South Sweden and provinces in the Baltic lands and Germany – was 6,831,761 dalers. Tax revenue was of course the crown's largest item of income.[57]

The proportion of donated land of the whole can also be given in tax-assessment units (*mantal*). In 1655 the proportion of the old and new donations was 65% of all tax assessment units in Sweden proper and 58% in Finland. The corresponding proportions for the old donations alone were 20% in Sweden and 5% in Finland.[58]

In any case, the interests of the crown and the nobility differed sharply with regard to ensuring the operation of the armed forces and the crown economy. A poorly waged war against Brandenburg and Denmark in 1674/5–1679 and an energetic monarch of majority age, Charles XI (1672–1697) were required for the requirements of the non-noble estates of a restitution to the crown of the donated taxes to change from propaganda into an explicit agenda for the government. In the same connection, autocratic rule was established in the realm.

As a result of the so-called grand restitution (*reduktion*) which began to be implemented in 1680, the economy of the Finnish provinces changed. By 1695, instalments in the Province of Åbo

---

[57]   RA, Kammararkivet, Kammarkollegiet, Generalbokhålleriet, Rikshuvudbok 1669, vol. 122 (KA, FR 1607). On the role of Finland in the economy of the realm in the 17th century, see Sven-Erik Åström, 'The Role of Finland in the Swedish National and War Economies during Sweden's Period as a Great Power,' *Scandinavian Journal of History* 1986, pp.135–147.

[58]   Jutikkala, *Bonden – adelsmannen – kronan*, pp. 13–14, 80.

51

and Björneborg (including the Åland Islands) totalled 159,967 silver dalers and crown expenditure was 257,577 dalers. The corresponding figures were 87,529 / 178,461 for the Province of Nyland and Tavastehus in 1694, 70,516 / 171,947 in the Province of Viborg in 1695, and 12,766 / 123,519 for the Province of Ostrobothnia in 1695 (instalments / crown expenditure).[59] The implementation of the restitution thus considerably expanded the taxational basis of the crown. However, the holdings restituted from the nobility to the crown often had unduly high taxes, for which reason tax relief had to be granted to them. Therefore in comparison with 1670 the number of all instalments had not decreased by 1695 as much as the amount of tax exemption on the basis of donation. The restitution did not apply to old donated properties of the nobility.

In the 17th century the vast majority of the Finnish population spoke Finnish as their mother tongue and only a minority, estimated at less than one-fifth[60], spoke Swedish. The latter lived on the western and southern coasts of Finland. The estates ranked above the peasants were completely or predominantly Swedish-speaking. Among the burghers there were some who spoke Finnish or German as their mother tongue. But even among the upper class some command of Finnish was common. The mother tongue of the peasants and the common people was of no significance for their social standing. Although the Finnish language had no official standing, all important crown decrees and declarations were read in Finnish from the pulpit in churches in Finnish-speaking parishes. The language spoken by the common people of the estates donated to the nobility and parishes mentioned in this study is not of importance for the questions explored here. It should be mentioned, however, that the Åland

---

[59]   KA, main calculations of the year in question (in general provincial ledgers).
[60]   Eino Jutikkala, 'Finlands befolkning och befolkande,' Historisk Tidskrift för Finland 1987, p. 369. The population of the Province of Kexholm was included in the total population of Finland.

Villnäs castle in Askais, Finland-Proper. The stone manor house was built in the 1650s by Herman Fleming who was the governor-general of Finland in 1664–1669. Born in 1619 at Villnäs, he was sent to Finland as the governor-general by the regency who wanted to get rid of an overly enthusiastic supporter of the restitution. Very few stone manor houses were erected in the 17th century Finland – only two remain today – while many more (e.g. Sjundby) had been built during the 16th century. This shows that Finland was increasingly considered as the periphery of the Swedish kingdom. Many members of the noble families of either Finnish origins or rooted in Finland preferred to serve in the centre of the realm in Stockholm and in Sweden, accumulating their landed property there. That is where the high nobility also built or acquired their stone castles. Villnäs was the birth home of C. G. E. Mannerheim (1867–1951), Marshal of Finland and President of the Republic. National Board of Antiquities.

Islands and the parishes of Pargas, Tenala, Sjundeå, Esbo, Helsinge, Sibbo and Borgå were either completely or predominantly Swedish speaking, while Bjärnå and Lojo were on the boundary of the language areas, and both languages were spoken there.

53

THE PEASANTS UNDER THE AUTHORITY OF THE NOBILITY

RENT FOR THE NOBILITY AND TAXES FOR THE CROWN

Information has survived concerning Hitå estate in the parish[61] of Sibbo and the annual rent paid by the peasants of the approximately 35 holdings (roughly 20 *mantal* tax-assessment units) belonging to it. The estate belonged to the heirs of Privy Councillor Jesper Matsson Cruus (his widow Brita De la Gardie). The Hitå cadastre covers the years 1639–1642 and 1643–1644. Approximately two-thirds of the peasant holdings were of the new donations (purchased donations and three holdings of eternal i.e. allodial donations) and the remaining third were old donations. Presumably most of the former had lost their hereditary rights. Comparing the rent paid by them in 1643–1644 with corresponding taxes in the provincial accounts[62], it can be seen that the tax articles had been thoroughly changed and the values in cash of the tax or rent employing so-called crown values in either cadastre

---

[61] The term parish here refers mainly to administrative parishes and not to the parishes of congregations.

[62] It is not possible to present comparisons with regard to the old donated properties, because the crown cadastre lists only uncertain, and later also extraordinary, taxes on their part, but not the annual rent, because they did not pay such tax to the crown even in theory.

do not correspond to each other. On the holdings near Hitå the value of the rent is only slightly or to a minor degree smaller than the crown's annual rent and uncertain taxes to which the rent should be compared. The general ledger (*landsbok*) of the crown for the Province of Nyland and Tavastehus shows that most of the rented farms of the Hitå estate did not pay uncertain taxes to the crown. In other words, they belong to the so-called boundary peasant holdings or those within the freedom mile that were exempted under the 1612/17 privileges granted by King Gustavus Adolphus (*rå och rörs- och frihetsmilshemman*). Only three holdings situated further away in the parish of Tusby paid a half share of their uncertain taxes to the crown. Therefore, the rent paid by two of them to the owner of Hitå was thus considerably less than the amount of the annual rent and uncertain taxes laid down in the crown cadastre. On the part of the third one, however, this was barely the case.

It is, however, obvious that the differences are not solely due to changes to the tax items or other technical matters. Instead the landlord had used his right to decree the rent paid by his tenants to the items and the level that suited both the owner and the tenants. The tenant farmers located further away from Hitå[63] were assigned the care of the landlord's livestock (inventory livestock), whereby the necessary labour, hay and feed were the invisible components of the rent, while the visible items consisted of the slaughtered animals and related produce deriving from the inventory livestock. In corresponding terms, it can be assumed that the tenants living near Hitå manor carried out daily labour services that were not recorded (this was no doubt also done by the more distant tenants but to a smaller degree). On the basis of the modest yield of Hitå manor (which in fact was a holding of only one-third of a *mantal* tax-assessment unit) the day-labour burden was small. On the other hand, the day-labour requirement could also have concerned the loading and transport of tax items

---

[63]   Some from even quite close.

and other produce of the Finnish holdings of the Cruus family to Sweden, because Hitå was a port site.

The rent of the old donated holdings belonging to Hitå was, according to the estate cadastre, 25.6 silver dalers per *mantal* assessment unit, and 29.9 silver dalers for the other i. e. new donated holdings. To the burden of the of the other donated holdings we must also add the half-shares of uncertain taxes paid to the crown by three holdings in Tusby, whereby the burden of payments per *mantal* assessment unit in the group rises to 30.6 silver dalers. Throughout the administrative district (*härad*) of Borgå, the tax burden for other than old donated properties (i.e. tax holdings, crown holdings and all other donated holdings) was 28.4 silver dalers per *mantal* assessment unit in 1644 according to the crown accounts.

Basing on these figures and bearing in mind the day-labour services that remained completely unrecorded, there is reason to assume that the rent payments of the donated tenants, with the exception of the old donated holdings, remained at approximately the same level as if the holdings had been bound to the crown. The tax-assessment unit figure of the holding naturally corresponded to its ability to pay tax to only an approximate degree, and this approximate nature makes the average rent-burden figures for the two groups of farms at Hitå somewhat uncertain particularly in view of the fact that the holdings in question total slightly less than 20 *mantal* tax-assessment units.

It is, however, claimed here that the above conclusion is probably correct, for among other reasons because it corresponds to the results obtained by Margareta Revera and Kurt Ågren according to which the rent of the old donated holdings (including labour services) were much smaller in the accounts than that of other holdings and even other donated holdings. It should be noted that not all of the day-labour services of the old donated holdings were even entered into the accounts. It is difficult to say whether this would explain the difference in the average burden among the groups of holdings at Hitå. Many of the old donated farms of the Hitå estate were, however, further away from the

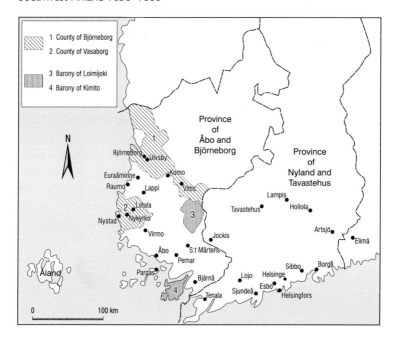

manor, which no doubt restricted opportunities to demand day-labour services.

It is yet a completely different matter whether or not the owner of Hitå manor was able to collect all that was he or she was entitled to according to the estate cadastre. In all regions of Finland, part of the tax and rent of holdings remained unpaid even in good years, not to mention times of crop failure. There is no information on the real rent yield and arrears of the Hitå estate. In any case, the rent of the Hitå tenant farmers was accommodated according to the solvency of the peasants, their actual produce and sales prospects, to approximately meet the level of crown taxation, except for the part of the old donated holdings, which no doubt had some encumbrances that were not recorded in the accounts.[64]

The position of the old donated estates and their tenants was most probably dictated by the old medieval concept that *Herrschaft* entailed a moral obligation based on mutual interests. Since the need for aid in each situation could not be known in advance, and was thus boundless in principle, there were no attempts to define it.[65] Therefore, also the crown did not register in the cadastre the supernumerary auxiliary taxes any more than certain labour services. It is also possible that the nobles left the total encumbrances of the tenants of the old donations smaller than those of other peasants under their authority, because the former were completely their peasants unlike the new donations whose taxes had only been donated and of whose encumbrances the crown still kept records as if to demonstrate that the donation could be revoked if necessary. Encumbrances that were lower

---

[64] Lunds universitetsbibiliotek (LUB), De la Gardieska arkivet, Topographica, Harviala, Nokia, Vik, Hitå och Sätuna gårdar, vol. 16, Årlig ränta och jordebok, Hitå gård, 1643–1644 (& 1639–1642) (KA, FR 764); KA, province accounts, the Province of Nyland and Tavastehus, 7926 (cadastre and general ledger 1644), 7946 (cadastre 1650) (the taxes in dalers for the properties are taken from the cadastre for 1650, 1661 and 1665); Revera, *Gods och gård 1650–1680*, pp. 41–62, 69–76; Ågren, *Adelns bönder och kronans*, pp. 117–194; Christer Kuvaja & Arja Rantanen, *Sibbo sockens historia*, I (Jyväskylä, 1994), pp. 156–157. On the privileges of the nobility, see Swenne, *Svenska adelns ekonomiska privilegier 1612–1651*. J. Köhn, the lessee of Porkkala manor in Lampis, responded to the complaint lodged against him by the peasants by claiming that it was the established custom for donated-land peasants who had lost their hereditary right to spin linen or hemp for their masters according to the needs of the latter. RA, Sävstaholmssamlingen I, Egendoms- och släkthandlingar, vol. 131, Nr. 39, 10.7.1693 (KA, FR 473). On Köhn's manorial economy, see Yrjö Koskinen, 'Muutamia lisä-tietoja nälkä-vuosista 1695–1697,' *Historiallinen Arkisto* 1 1866, pp. 73–89. In calculating the rents for Hitå and Meltola crown values are used, as also in the accounts. The above-mentioned accounts for Nokia and Harviala are in produce, and owing to the lack of total sums in ready money and the large number of properties belonging to them, it is laborious to convert them into money.

[65] Brunner, *Land und Herrschaft*, pp. 269–303; Reinholdsson, *Uppror eller resningar?*, pp. 200–201. The master's need for assistance had to have due grounds; unfounded auxiliary taxes could be contested. Temporary auxiliary taxes were better suited to the peasant than permanent raises in rent.

than for other parties suggested at least in theory that that the old donated-land peasants were close to the heart of the landlord and enjoyed his particular protection. A practical consideration, the reserve ensured by undefined resources, was masked at the level of ideology as an indication of the particular favour of the landlord.

Information on rent paid by the donated-land peasants to their landlords is also available on approximately 70 holdings and over 30 *mantal* tax-assessment units (according to the situation prevailing at the turn of the 1640s and 1650s) belonging to Gerknäs and Sjundby manors owned by Count[66] Clas Tott in the parishes of Lojo and Sjundeå respectively. The accounts are quite mixed in nature, because the lists of rent paid by the holdings were drawn up mainly in view of their sale or pledging. In the management of their own economic affairs, Clas Åkesson Tott (born 1630) and his stepmother Christina Brahe were not capable of making both ends meet. For a number of reasons, not all of Tott's ownings can be identified in the crown cadastres. In the Tott cadastre the tax units for annual rent and the *mantal* assessment units of some holdings differ from the corresponding crown figures.

In the Tott cadastre the "donated holdings" (*"frälsehemman"*) are marked with a higher rent in relation to their assessment units than the "tax holdings" (*"skattehemman"*). Their higher rent was mainly due to the fact that the inventory livestock of the manor was located on them. This fact defined the "donated holdings", since they included both tax holdings and ones that had lost their hereditary rights. Moreover, it became apparent after Tott's period that the peasants often had a different idea of the preservation of the hereditary rights than the manor had. Animals for slaughter raised the value of the rent, although in reality the peasant's own contribution consisted of the work needed for tending the animals, and hay and feed. Also in this

---

[66]   From 1652; appointed privy councillor in 1653.

The construction of Sjundby manor house in the parish of Sjundeå started in the 1560s. Clas Tott (1630–1674) sold the manor in 1654 to no less than Queen Christina herself. Tott lavishly spent most of the inheritance (including Gerknäs estate in Lojo) of his family, originally from Denmark but rooted in Finland. Clas's father Åke Tott had served with success during the Thirty Years' War, dying in 1640 at the early age of 42. Thanks to his father's merits and Queen Christina's favouritism, Tott became a count in 1652 at the age of 22. His county Karleborg comprised part of Southern Ostrobothnia. Sjundby is situated in the area of the Porkkala peninsula, leased by the Soviet Union as their military base during the aftermath of WW2 (1944–1956). National Board of Antiquities.

situation the landlord had with sovereign right arranged the rent in a manner different from the crown cadastre in keeping with his own interests and the actual agricultural work of the farms.

The rent (annual rent) was generally less than the annual rent and uncertain taxes laid down in the crown cadastre, but in some cases it exceeded the latter. On the other hand, the rent of farms that were in difficulties had been markedly lowered in comparison to the corresponding crown taxes. This situation is shown by the Tott cadastres of 1645 and 1666 in the Swedish National Archives. Owing to land transactions carried out by the Totts, these documents were by no means identical. In 1654 Clas Tott sold Sjundby manor to Queen Christina of Sweden (reigned 1644– 1654 – the queen helped her favourite with this purchase). Sjundby was subsequently donated to new masters, and in 1660 it was bought by Baron Ernst Johan Creutz, governor of the Province of Nyland and Tavastehus. In 1666 Gerknäs was obtained from Tott by the former's brother, Baron and Privy Councillor Lorentz Creutz the Elder (and two years later by Herman Fleming, governor-general of Finland).

In addition to the rent there were also the day-labour services, the amount of which was regulated by the crown only for the peasants who had preserved their hereditary rights (since 1652). According to the cadastre of 1654 for Sjundby manor, five peasants or holdings provided 12 days of work per year, while one peasant served 18 days. According to the landlord, they still had their hereditary rights. The others had to serve the manor two days per week in the summer. In E. J. Creutz's cadastre (from 1658 or later) the peasants of Sjundby were now expected to pay not only the annual rent but also the uncertain taxes, which raised the total rent sum by one fifth or one third according to the method of calculation. According to the cadastre the peasants, however, paid their uncertain taxes in day-labour services, which meant that there had been no real change with regard to conditions during Tott's period. In theory, however, the total rent burden of the peasants of Sjundby was now higher than the rent according to the crown cadastre. Creutz's intention does not appear to have been to raise the rent of the peasants in bookkeeping terms, but to make all the peasants, including the tax peasants, to provide more day-labour services. As a definite price was attached to the day-labour services, it became increasingly difficult for the peasants to refuse to perform them.

During Creutz's period in the early 1670s the day-labour obligations of the tenant farmers of Sjundby were raised by resorting to a falsification of documents. In this situation, peasants were deprived of their hereditary rights on the basis of tax arrears in order to raise the amount of day-labour services provided by them.

There is also the Tott cadastre of 1641 (in the National Archives of Sweden). This document concerns holdings in wilderness parishes of the provinces of Tavastia and Satakunta, as well as properties in the provinces of Viborg and Kexholm. A comparison of the former with the crown cadastres shows that the rent demanded by Tott was almost consistently higher than the crown taxes. This point may not merit too much emphasis, because the "raise in the rent" may only have been nominal and intended to raise the price of the holdings that were for sale. But there is also the alternative that Tott´s financial administration regarded the crown tax level in the inland to be too low, and sought to improve the yield of the holdings with an overall raise in payments.[67]

[67]   RA, Tottska samligen, Clas Tott, Godshandlingar, Gerknäs, Sjundby et al., E 5818 (vol. 38, KA, FR 219); KA, Province of Nyland and Tavastehus, 7946, 7971 & 7985 (1650, 1661, 1665), Province of Åbo and Björneborg , 7261 & 7294 (1661, 1665). Some of the Tott properties are listed as old donations, even though the crown accounts show that he did not have such ownings in the parish concerned. The nobility was often insufficiently aware of the specific nature of their properties and at times the mistakes were deliberate. Owing to his age and need to travel, Clas Tott did not begin to administer his lands until 1652. Alf Brenner, *Sjundeå sockens historia,* I (Hangö, 1953), pp. 282–295; Heikki Ylikangas, *Lohjalaisten historia,* I (Helsinki, 1973), p. 215; KA, Sjundby gårds arkiv I, Årlig ränta 1654 (This copy corresponds quite well to the 1645 cadastre in the Swedish National Archives in Stockholm), Jordebok 1658 (?). The Finnish National Archives also contains documents of the neighbouring manors of Svidja and Pickala from the 1660s: Topographica II, Sjundeå 4. The inventory livestock of the hereditary peasants sometimes consisted of their former animals, which the manor had seized in compensation for unpaid rent. See John Gardberg, *Kimito friherreskap: En studie över feodal läns- och godsförvaltning* (Helsingfors, 1935), pp. 177–178.

The peasants of Count[68] Gustav Carlsson Horn's purchased donation estate at Meltola in the parish of Pemar (total 20 *mantal* tax-assessment units) had been classed as old and new tenant farmers, presumably primarily because only the former had inventory livestock belonging to the manor. In 1650 the rent (annual rent) of the old tenants was higher than the annual crown rent, without the proportion of the inventory livestock given to them, the proceeds of which in slaughtered animals and products went to the landlord (while the proceeds after the deduction of costs for the care and upkeep of the livestock were for the tenant). On the other hand, with the proportion of the inventory livestock included, the annual rent was barely smaller than the sum of the crown's annual rent and uncertain taxes. The manor did not make the old tenants pay any of the latter.

The annual rent of the new tenants was almost the same as the crown's annual rent, to which it was attempted to be compared. In addition, they paid the uncertain taxes, which were also to be paid to the manor. The privileges granted to the nobility in 1644 had freed all donated land (now including other holdings than the boundary and freedom mile farms which had already been exempted) from the uncertain taxes. It is almost certain that in tending the inventory livestock the old tenants provided at least as much for the landlord as they had gained through slightly lower rent. In addition, there were also the day-labour services. According to the financial records of 1631, the tenants had been required to provide these services up to three times (three days) a week.[69]

---

[68]   Since 1651. Military commander in the Thirty Years' War, appointed Marshal of the Realm in 1653.

[69]   RA, Bielkesamlingen, Gustav Horn och Sigrid Bielke, Gods- och länshandlingar, Meltola gård, Jordebok 1650 (1653, 1661), Räkenskap 1631, E 2428 (vol. 32, KA, FR 202); KA, 7261 & 7294; Ågren, *Adelns bönder och kronans*, pp. 11–13. Meltola was a storage and loading site for goods shipped to Sweden and this required day-labour services. According to Jutikkala, half of the yield of the inventory livestock was paid in rent to the master. Jutikkala, 'Väestö ja yhteiskunta,' p. 314.

In the County (*grevskap*) of Björneborg, the County of Vasaborg consisting of the main parts of the parishes of Nykyrko and Letala, and Bjärnå manor (*Bjärnå ladugård* or *Näsegård*), rent was paid in principle to the amount laid down in the crown cadastre.[70] The above shows that although the nobles could in individual cases make exceptions to the crown taxes in their rent, the latter were, with certain exceptions, the upper limit of the rent collected by the nobles. What the nobles granted in the rent of holdings capable of paying taxes, they would try to recover in the form of day-labour services.

Count[71] Per Brahe, governor-general of Finland in the years 1637–1640 and 1648—1651/54, clearly differed from the practice whereby rents were not raised above the level of the crown taxes. In 1648 at Juva manor in the parish of S:t Mårtens, in Count Per Brahe's donated lands in Finland-Proper, so-called contractual rent (*stadgeränta*) was decreed. In S:t Mårtens and at Brahe's holdings in the parish of Pargas, the hay, or later cash (S:t Mårtens) or barrels of Baltic herring (Pargas), to be paid in addition to the rent to compensate for day labour, raised the rent, particularly in Pargas, to a clearly higher level than the corresponding annual rent, uncertain taxes and half-payments of livestock fees. When ruling on day-labour services (i.e. on compensation for them), Brahe, the supporter of aristocratic rule, bypassed the question of the peasant's hereditary rights or the lack thereof as irrelevant.

At Juva manor in S:t Mårtens as many as over half of its holdings and *mantal* tax-assessment units were abandoned (i.e. unable to pay taxes) or were granted other forms of officially recognized

---

70   In the years 1649–1652 the rulings of the queen and the *Riksdag* underscored the view that the crown cadastre also defined the level of the tax peasants' taxes even when they were under the authority of the nobles. Jutikkala, *Bonden i Finland genom tiderna*, pp. 165–166, 170; Katajala, *Suomalainen kapina*, pp. 240–252, 291–307. These rulings and the underlying pressure exerted by the non-noble estates apparently had the effect that the rent laid down on the properties in the accounts of the nobles now approached the crown tax payments, albeit there were major differences among the noble estates, as has been seen.

71   Privy councillor, Justiciar of the Realm etc.

64

ILLVSTRIS; AC GENEROSISSIMVS HEROS, DN;DN: GVSTAVVS HORN

Master of the County of Björneborg and of the manors of Esbogård and Meltola, Marshal of the Realm, Count Gustav Carlsson Horn (1592–1657). Copperplate. National Board of Antiquities.

exemption from the payment of taxes between 1648 and 1662, which means that in practice the total of some 100 *mantal* assessment units in S:t Mårtens produced less than half their number in Pargas. In the one-quarter restitution in 1663 Brahe gave the Pargas and S:t Mårtens donations back to the crown, but

Count and later Justiciar of the Realm Per Brahe the younger (1602–1680) was evicted twice from the top cabinets of the kingdom to "cool down" in Finland where he served as governor-general. In the 1630s he was sent to Finland by Chancellor of the Realm Axel Oxenstierna and his supporters, while in the following decade he was virtually expelled by Queen Christina, now of age. The achievements of Brahe include the founding of Åbo academy (university) in 1640. In the report compiled at the end of his first mandate, Brahe wrote that the Province of Kexholm and the parts of Ostrobothnia facing the Russian border were "only stone", thus particularly weak areas from an economic point of view. Almost a spite, in 1650 he was given the Barony of Kajana which was situated precisely in this area. Brahe was an unwavering advocate of the supremacy of the nobility. In the regency which served during the young years of King Charles XI, he represented the voice of experience. National Board of Antiquities / Timo Syrjänen.

took the best holdings in S:t Mårtens and his Pargas donations as his benefices (*beställning*) for his post of Justiciar of the Realm (*riksdrots*). Where 34.6% of all the *mantal* assessment units in S:t Mårtens Parish were abandoned in 1663, only one out of ten assessment units at Brahe's benefice holdings were in this form of non-tax paying state there. At the same time the contractual rent of the S:t Mårtens benefices was adjusted, mostly in a higher direction, apparently to compensate for the day-labour services that were now no longer included. The contractual rent in S:t Mårtens and Pargas (including the day-labour fish in the latter) respectively were 14.6% and ca. 16–18% (depending on the method of calculation) higher than the corresponding taxes paid by these holdings according to the crown cadastre. This, however, was not the only disadvantage for the peasants, for owing to the change in their status, the benefices of S:t Mårtens and Pargas also had to pay the remaining half of their livestock fees (i.e. the whole fee instead of the former half) to the crown but the contractual rent paid to the Justiciar of the Realm was not lowered on account of it. The salary income of the Justiciar coming from S:t Mårtens and Pargas consisted only of annual rent and uncertain taxes. In other words, Brahe was no longer entitled to receive the half-payments of livestock fees, but in practice he kept at least the corresponding sum. Brahe thus served his own interests at all stages, and neither did the crown fail to benefit in the conversion to benefices. All this can be called excellent tax planning, with which other nobles or Brahe's peasants did not dare to interfere because of Brahe's high position.[72]

---

[72]   RA, Brahesamlingen, Per Brahe d.y., Finska godshandlingar, Räkenskaper & jordeböcker 1648–1656, Pargas & Juva gård, St Mårtens, E 3323–3324, 3328 (vols 23–24, 28, KA, FR 203–205); RA, Rydboholmssamlingen, Brev till Per Brahe d.y., vol. 13, Sven Månsson 30.4.1663 (KA, FR 214); RA, Kammararkivet, Grev- och friherreskap, Kajana, Räkenskaper 1662 (KA, FR 313); KA, 7262, 7289, 7294, 7295, 9139, 9140, 9149. Even after the one-quarter restitution, Brahe had a number of donated properties in Pargas. On Per Brahe as governor-general of Finland: Karonen, *Pohjoinen suurvalta*, pp 240–243.

Finally a few examples of the rent and related organization of affairs of the old donated lands (*gammalt frälse*). Firstly, the Porkkala holding in Lampis Parish, for whose donated-land peasants an old estate cadastre laid down rent in barrels of grain and the later cadastre of 1689 in several different items of produce.[73] Since the holdings mostly belonged to the old donated lands there was no comparable crown tax for them in the crown cadastre, especially since the 1678 crown cadastre indicated that some of the properties belonging to Porkkala manor had previously been kept outside the crown cadastre, where they did not even have a designation or *mantal* tax-assessment unit (i.e. not even their uncertain taxes had been set).[74] At the manors of Kiala and Boegård in the parish of Borgå there were crofters (*torpare*) in the actual *säter* manor area and its boundary zone during the last quarter of the century. In 1675 the crofters of Kiala compensated all their rent throughout the year by providing day-labour services all week long. They had to have several people in their households, because in the summer the labour services of two persons (not necessarily men) and a horse were required daily. The winter requirement was one person (or one man) and a horse every day.[75] The manors of Järnböle and Hornhattula

---

73 RA, Sävstaholmssamlingen I, vol. 131, Nr. 11, Jordebok över Porkkala gårds underliggande frälsebönder, Nr. 18, Jordebok uppå Baronen Carl Horns under Porkkala liggande bönder 1689 (KA, FR 473).

74 KA, 8022, pp. 294–295.

75 RA, Barthold Ruuths arkiv, Godshandlingar, Nylands och Tavastehus län, Jordebok uppå Kiala gård 1675, Jordebok eller rusttjänstlängd 1696, E 5235 (vol. 12, KA, FR 483–484); Anders Allardt, *Borgå sockens historia*, I (Helsingfors, 1925), pp. 175–188. KA, Topographica II, Borgå socken, Boegård II, contains the ledger of 1700–1710 for Boegård manor (including Kiala), which is slightly too late for the present study. The situation at Kiala was close to the ideal type of the so-called *Gutsherrschaft*, the opposite of which was *Grundherrschaft* (land domain or *seigneurie*), which implies the landlord's right of ownership and /or legal rights to a number of peasant properties. The landlord's income consisted of rent paid in money and produce; in complete *Grundherrschaft* even the manor was rented to be farmed by tenants (e.g. in *métayage*). In *Gutsherrschaft*, the yield of the manor was based on the day labour of the subordinate peasants, i.e. the peasant holdings belonging to it benefited it indirectly. The size of the noble estate grew and its yield was oriented towards export. East European *Gutsherrschaft* was associated with the judicial authority of the landlord over the peasants and with serfdom.

also in the parish of Borgå were under a sharecropping arrangement (*hälftenbruk / métayage*) in 1676.[76]

INTERACTION ON THE ESTATES OF THE NOBILITY: BJÄRNÅ MANOR

Näsegård, or *Bjärnå ladugård*[77] was obtained in 1642 by Count[78] Carl Gustav Wrangel and at its largest it consisted of approximately 70 holdings and 60 *mantal* tax-assessment units, most of them in Bjärnå Parish in the Province of Åbo and Björneborg, and the rest in Tenala Parish in the Province of Nyland and Tavastehus. Owing to the origins of the manor as a crown manor, most of its holdings were former crown holdings, i.e. lacking hereditary rights. Wrangel controlled this property either as donation according to the Norrköping resolution or as a so-called purchased donation. The cadastre from 1655, according to which the rent was collected gave the rent of the peasants in individual items. In the same manner as at Hitå and under Tott the items did not correspond to

---

Grundherrschaft was by nature *Rentengrundherrschaft* (tenancy authority). The peasants were subordinate to more than one kind of authority and they were not serfs. The Finnish noble estates had a varying amount of features pertaining to both ideal types. Quite complete *Grundherrschaft* was quite common. Heide Wunder, 'Das Selbstverständliche denken,' *Gutsherrschaft als soziales Modell: Vergleichende Betrachtungen zur Funktionsweise frühzeitlicher Agrargesellschaften*, Jan Peters (ed.), Historische Zeitschrift, Beiheft 18 (München, 1995), p. 23–24 (and the whole content of the latter); Porskrug Rasmussen, 'Godssystemer i Sønderjylland fra 1500- til 1700-tallet,' pp. 38, 57–58; Revera, *Gods och gård 1650–1680*, pp. 23–24, 61–62. Jutikkala, *Bonden – adelsmannen – kronan*, pp. 41, 66–67. The croft was a part of the holding that was cultivated under rent; it was not officially separated from the holding and it did not have its own *mantal* designation in the cadastre. These features distinguished it from the peasant holding. In the 17th century crofts were mostly established on the lands of the nobility in response to needs for labour, i.e. on a day-labour basis.

[76] RA, Barthold Ruuths arkiv, vol. 11, E 5234; Allardt, *Borgå sockens historia*, I, pp. 329–334. On the sharecropping system, see note 45.

[77] Gabriel Nikander & Eino Jutikkala, *Säterier och storgårdar i Finland*, II (Helsingfors, s.a.), pp. 345–349.

[78] From 1651. Military commander of the Thirty Years' War and the wars of King Charles X Gustav (1654–1660), privy councillor, governor-general of Pomerania.

those used in the crown cadastre, nor were the cash amounts of the rent completely the same as for the crown (annual rent and uncertain taxes) but an approximate correspondence had already been sought in Bjärnå in 1655.[79]

Already at the beginning of Wrangel's donation period two labour days per week were demanded from each peasant.[80] The day-labour requirement particularly concerned the peasants of the nearby vicinity. Per Skarp, bailiff of Bjärnå manor from the mid-1650s, demanded labour services three, and even four, days a week with reference to demands that he had received from Stockholm to deliver more goods and produce there. Skarp treated the peasants in a strict and violent manner. In 1662 the Swedish head office of Wrangel's donated properties carried out an investigation of complaints filed by peasants against Skarp, who only confessed to having once thrown a dry fir branch at a peasant; he had also beaten and sent home farm-maids and young boys who had been sent to work instead of able-bodied men. As was often the cases in these situations, the inquiry was not impartial, and the peasants were pressured to withdraw their complaints. One Bertil of Hästö, who had sent a complaint to Wrangel, was not even present at the inquiry – presumably out of fear. But in 1663–1664 the office had enough of the self-willed and violent bailiff. His accounts were inspected in great detail and a number of errors were found that were in favour of the bailiff and causing losses for Wrangel. The bailiff was thus felled by his own despotism and the complaints of the peasants.[81]

---

79   RA, Rydboholmssamlingen, Wrangelska godshandlingar, Bjärnå, Jordebok (cadastre) 1655 in connection with the accounts for that year, vol. 549, E 8015 (The letters concerning Bjärnå are on microfilm FR 215 and the other documents concerning the estate on FR 216–217, KA).

80   RA, Rydboholmssamlingen, Herman Wrangels arrendekontrakt 4.5.1642, vol. 548, E 8014.

81   RA, Rydboholmssamlingen, Rannsakning 15.1.1662 and letters of complaint in the same connection, vol. 548, E 8014, Underdånig relation 1663 & Nils Hisinghs rannsakning 15.8.1664, vol. 549, E 8015. On Skarp, see also Veikko Litzen, *Perniön historia*, 1 (Salo, 1980), pp. 247–248.

A medieval royal estate, Bjärnå manor was taken over by Carl Gustav Wrangel in the 1640s. Wrangel was involved in warfare in Germany and had no time to dedicate to household issues but his father, Marshal and Privy Councillor Herman Wrangel took care of his affairs in the early 1640s. The manor was situated close to the great Åbo-Viborg coastal road and to a rapid, and had long been the centre of many types of economic activities. In 1655 the manor also had two donkeys, something that the commoners had never seen – asses on four legs are still very rare in Finland. During restitution, the Crown repossessed the manor which later became one with the responsibility to provide for horsemen. The present main building dates back to the 18th century but many alterations have been made to the facade and building itself. Photo: Eric Sundström. National Board of Antiquities.

The majority of the peasants of Bjärnå had lost their hereditary rights, and with regard to day labour services were in a much weaker situation than the tax peasants of the donated lands (*skattefrälsebönder*). In 1653 Esbogård manor, in the possession of Gustav Horn, had 32 tax peasants. The manor proposed one labour day per week in winter and two in summer, which would

71

have been recompensed with a relatively small reduction in the rent and the halving of the burden of providing sailors for the navy. The peasants did not agree to this, and accordingly they had to be granted the relatively limited day-labour services laid down for tax peasants by the *Riksdag* the year before (18 labour days per year from a whole farm) without reduction of rent.[82] On the other hand, the crown had left peasants lacking hereditary rights without the protection of legislation to haggle with their respective manors over the amount of day-labour services.

Accordingly, in 1689 the district court session at Euraåminne ordered the peasants of Vuojoki manor, who had lost their hereditary rights, to carry out their day-labour services obediently and to accept the fact that a bull had been confiscated from each of them for missing day labour. The court maintained that the labour requirement was not unduly high, as claimed by the peasants, but was to be freely decided upon by the landlord. The lessee Johan Nordman was entitled to put vociferously complaining peasants in handcuffs, because the landlord, Major-General Axel Wachtmeister[83] had given such orders for cases of insubordination. The landlord has also authorized the lessee to lock disobedient peasants in the manor's own dungeon, which Nordman, however, did not do. The existence of a dungeon, both here and in many other manors showed that manorial discipline was very strict. In legal terms, manorial justice, i.e. the right of the landlord to punish peasants, existed only from 1671 to 1675, but in practice it was applied and followed extensively.[84]

---

[82]   RA, Wijksamlingen, Gustav Horn och Sigrid Bielke, Ankomna brev, Hans Hansson Gode to G. Horn 22.9.1653, E 2820 (vol. 82, KA, FR 221).

[83]   Count since 1693, a favourite of King Charles XI (1672–1697).

[84]   KA, judicial district of Lower Satakunta II, judgment book 1689, p. 443 (Euraåminne autumn district court sessions 5.–8.10.1689). If the value of seized oxen exceeded that of undone day labour, the surplus was to be returned to the peasants. Also Ulla Heino, *Eurajoen historia*, I (Jyväskylä, 1987), pp. 134–138, 169, 171–172, 182–184. Wachtmeister ultimately discharged Nordman for placing too much strain on the tenants, in other words, appeals from the peasants to their landlord residing away from the manor led to results. On manorial jurisdiction, see Jutikkala, *Bonden i Finland genom tiderna*, p. 172.

It was traditionally marked in the crown records that the peasants of Bjärnå manor, whose land consisted of 29 holdings and *mantal* tax-assessment units, paid uncertain taxes to only half a *mantal* unit, i.e. according to 14.5 *mantal* units.[85] The manor's cadastre of 1655, already mentioned above, laid down the rent on this basis. In the same year, however, Wrangel´s Swedish office drew up a new cadastre in which full uncertain taxes and also extraordinary taxes were decreed also for the boundary farms of Bjärnå manor (the 28 holdings and *mantal* units mentioned above). On the part of the extraordinary taxes, the manor recorded for itself everything that the crown had ceased to levy. The purpose was no doubt to see how much more the manor could produce and on a suitable occasion carry out such plans. In principle, the manor was entitled to raise rent and tax in such a manner, because the boundary peasants paid only poll-tax to the crown. The raise, however, "forgot" the rent paid by the peasants in labour to the manor.[86]

From 1663 onwards rent began to be collected on raised grounds. The raise was in force for approximately five years. In 1668 the manor was leased to regimental clerk Johan Jacob Lundh. The annual lease sum was set at 1,600 silver dalers, i.e. the rent (taxes) of the peasants appended to the manor. The lessee was entitled to keep any other income from the estate (including proceeds from day-labour services). The peasants, however, now complained about the increase. Wrangel, or his office, had to admit that the complaint was justified and the raise in rent was cancelled (except for half of the extraordinary taxes, which the manor had not yet levied in the 1650s). It is obvious that the uncertain taxes were originally halved in compensation for the

[85] KA, 7261 & 7262 (cadastre and general ledger 1656).

[86] RA, Rydboholmssamlingen, Jordebok 1655 in connection with accounts for that year (actual collection), vol. 549, E 8015, Jordebok 1655, vol. 550, E 8016. The documents of the estate include several undated cadastres or rent lists, or ones dated to 1649, which appear to be from the 1660s and provide grounds for raising rent. KA, 7294 & 7305 (cadastre 1665, 1668).

large amount day labour required from the peasants. During Lundh's period the manor returned to the original situation, and in addition the lessee had to make do with only one labour day per week because of the resistance of the peasants.

This victory, however, did not mean that the peasants were now freed from under the domination of their landlords. In the inquiry of 1669 they were pressured to break ranks with Erik Bertilsson of Hästö, who had lodged a complaint in their name concerning Lundh. According to the inquiry, Erik Bertilsson, who was possibly the son of Bertil of Hästö, the earlier complainant, had neglected the care of his holding and his day-labour services, and a harder-working man was now needed to replace him. Lundh thus tried to take revenge on Erik for having given him the role of Skarp. According to a crown list of arrears from 1676 Erik was a beggar, but it is impossible to tell from the available sources whether Lundh, who was lessee from 1668 to 1671 and again after 1675, had actually evicted him.

In conjunction with the dismissal of Skarp and the leasing of the manor, the office had clearly sought new economic benefits for Wrangel. The annual lease sum laid down for Lundh was 1,600 silver dalers, which was approximately equivalent to the rents of all the appended peasants (including those beyond the boundary) amounting to 1,620 silver dalers, but as it was necessary to lower the uncertain taxes, the lease also had to be lowered to 1,400 dalers.[87] The benefit from the increase would thus have gone to Wrangel and not to Lundh. Even in the 1650s and in 1661

---

[87]   RA, Rydboholmssamlingen, C. G. Wrangels ekonomiska brevväxling, H. Andersson to C. G. Wrangel, "Presenterat Stockholm 14.10.1668," vol. 486, E 7952, Arrendekontrakt 12.9.1667, J. J. Lundhs memorial "Alldenstund" 10.6.1669, letter "Presenterat Stockholm 26.10.1668," G. Melartopaeus' memorial 2.–4.5.1668, Rannsakning 20.12.1669, vol. 548, E 8014, Gårds- och specialräkningar 1664–1667, Jordebok 1663, 1664 and several undated or incorrectly dated cadastres from the 1660s, Årliga räntan och gärden 1668 (in which the rent again corresponds to the crown cadastre), vols 549–550, E 8015–8016; KA, 7294 (cadastre 1665). Erik Bertilsson: 7336, p. 1854, 7311, p. 758, 7314, p. 1128.

the rent paid by the peasants (without extraordinary taxes) was totally only slightly less than 1,200 dalers,[88] which meant that the increase was considerable, particularly since it concerned only part of the peasants.

When Skarp had to resign, the peasants of Bjärnå manor had rent in arrears to the amount 2,700–2,800 silver dalers, which had to be pardoned, without Wrangel receiving a single penny of the sum. According to the calculations of his office in Sweden, the manor had nonetheless during Skarp's period as bailiff in 1655–1663 provided the count in Sweden with approximately 8,560 dalers for his needs, an average of 950 dalers per annum according to Stockholm prices.[89] Not only farmed and animal produce but also various building materials were sent from Bjärnå to Sweden, all of which required day-labour services from the peasants. The fact that there were proceeds from the estate (manor) even in years of crop failure, not to mention good years, explains why Wrangel and other noblemen could live with the perennial arrears of the peasants. They did their best to collect them, but owing to the repeated years of poor crops their means were often limited.[90] But day labour was not left in arrears here, or anywhere else; the nobles always received what they were entitled to, or at least what they needed.

In one of the memoranda of Bjärnå manor it was proposed that the peasants who accumulated arrears were to be evicted from their holdings and replaced by more suitable ones, but at least according to the accounts and other documents of the estate, action was taken to obtain the hereditary rights of only one peasant

---

88   RA, Rydboholmssamlingen, Jordebok 1655 & Per Joensson Skarps räkenskap 1661, vol. 549, E 8015.

89   RA, Rydboholmssamlingen, Underdånig relation 1663, Rydboholmssamlingen, vol. 549, E 8015.

90   The sum of the list of arrears for the above-mentioned Esbogård manor was 2,391 silver dalers in 1661 and 4,203 silver dalers in 1667. Owing to changes in the exchange rates of currency (the decrease in value of copper coinage), the arrears grew even more in reality. RA, Bielkesamlingen, Gustav Horn och Sigrid Bielke, Gods- och länshandlingar, Esbo gård, E 2427 (vol. 31, KA, FR 201).

in the village of Koskis in Tenala Parish, and to evict him.[91] As there were abandoned holdings in all parts and it was difficult to find new farmers for them even with the means of temporary exemption from tax or rent, neither the crown nor the nobles could afford mass evictions. The wars of the realm maintained a permanent shortage of labour.

In 1670 Wrangel had to grant a 19% reduction (*förmedling*) for the total rent of his peasants, which applied to the farmers in the worst difficulties. In other words, it was unrealistic to imagine that it was possible to collect all rent in full. On the contrary, reductions had to be granted.[92] In this respect Wrangel not only acknowledged fact but also followed the model of a good and just landlord. In the 1670s the total rent of the peasants of Bjärnå (without the effect of arrears) amounted to barely more than a thousand silver dalers, and when the manor was again leased from 1675 onwards, the lease sum was set at a thousand silver dalers.[93] The manor's most productive years were thus hopelessly a thing of the past. The crop failures of the 1670s were a strain on farmers, manors and the crown both here[94] and in all parts of Finland.

Wrangel and those subordinate to him and the peasants of Bjärnå manor thus sought to benefit at the cost of others, the manor by seeking higher rent and more day labour and the peasants through complaints and other pressure (by demonstrating

---

[91]   RA, Rydboholmssamlingen, Tjänstl. relation, vol. 486, E 7952, Årliga räntan och gärden 1668 m. bil., Restlängd 1671–1674, Bjärnågårdens arrende 1675, vol. 550, E 8016. Most of the manor's peasants already lacked hereditary rights and they could easily be evicted because neglect of obligations. A similar recommendation to give notice to peasants in arrears is given in resolution 18.8.1664, in response to questions presented by Henrik Larsson, lessee of Sjundby manor. RA, Tottska samlingen, Clas Tott, E 5818 (vol. 38, KA, FR 219). The question of losing hereditary rights to the nobles is discussed further below.

[92]   RA, Rydboholmssamlingen, Uträkning 1670–1671, vol. 550, E 8016.

[93]   RA, Rydboholmssamlingen, Arrendekontrakt 10.6.1675, vol. 548, E 8014, accounts of the 1670s, vol. 550, E 8016.

[94]   RA, Rydboholmssamlingen, Bjärnå, Ordinarie härads vinterting 27.–28.1.1679, vol. 548, E 8014.

their unwillingness). The complaints of the latter were often noted to be contrary to the truth or at least exaggerated, but it was the underlying logic of the complaints and appeals to exaggerate in order to draw attention to real problems. The peasants regarded the bailiff or lessee of the manor, not the count, as the source of their problems. In part, they may have actually thought in these terms, and partly not. Both parties utilized the role game of a just landlord and his faithful tenants.[95] But even for the nobles the model of the just landlord was not necessarily a charade, but an obligation which one took to heart – as Wrangel certainly did – or not. On the other hand, he or those who administrated his property liked to test whether the peasants would accept raises in rent and encumbrances. Economic benefits would easily put high moral principles in second place. It is no less insufficient to explain the actions of peasants or their aristocratic landlords solely in terms of rational calculations of profit or ideology; both aspects played a part.

It is not known how much time Wrangel, a leading dignitary of Swedish realm, had to study the affairs of a relatively peripheral manorial property such as Bjärnå, but regardless of whether the complaints of the peasants were resolved by the count himself or his administrators, it must be acknowledged that complaints accompanied by pressure were anything but useless activity for the peasants. There are thus grounds to speak of interaction between completely unequal parties. Wrangel had to follow the same policy as the crown, i.e. recognize the social contract formed by the encumbrances marked in the cadastre for each farm.

---

[95] Scott, *Weapons of the Weak*, keyword Compliance and conformity (p. 377).

THE COUNTY OF BJÖRNEBORG:
INTERACTION AND RESTORED DISCIPLINE

In 1651 the County of Björneborg was donated to Gustav Horn. It consisted of some 370 holdings (designations) and 230 *mantal* units in the parishes of Ulvsby, Kumo and Vittis, augmented by the purchased tax-donation estate of Vampula (ca. 50 holdings and 30 *mantal* units). After the death of Count Gustav Horn in 1657 the property went to his spouse, Sigrid Bielke. Two histories of the County of Björneborg have been written[96], and it is sufficient here only to discuss the most important points for the subject at hand.

In principle, the peasants of the county paid their rent according to the crown cadastre. But this was no benefit for the peasant at least in situations where increased day-labour obligations were added to unreduced rent.[97] On the other hand, arrears in rent always made the increased rent burden of the peasants only more or less theoretical. As the county, i. e. the count's donated property, consisted of only a reasonable proportion of all holdings in the respective parishes (the majority only in Vittis), it could not monopolize related accounting in its area and almost exclude the crown, as had been the case for example in the County of Vasaborg. The peasants who had lost their hereditary rights were ordered to provide as much day labour as required by the count's domain.[98] Apparently in this respect the situation was satisfactory for the county and it did not have to increase the day-labour services of its large area. Accordingly, the county did not seek to systematically obtain the hereditary rights of the peasants who

---

[96] Mauno Jokipii, 'Porin kreivikunta,' *Historiallinen Arkisto* 54 1953, pp. 105–169; Janne Haikari, *Suurläänitys – perintötilallisen uhka?: Läänityslaitos Huittisissa 1638–1679*, unpublished MA thesis in Finnish history, University of Jyväskylä. See also Jokipii, *Suomen kreivi- ja vapaaherrakunnat*, I–II (Helsinki, 1956, 1960), passim.

[97] If day labour was not recorded in any way, it could in principle be just as well in addition to other rent as replacing part of it.

[98] Haikari, *Suurläänitys – perintötilallisen uhka?*, p. 44.

were in arrears with rent.[99] Day-labour services were provided for the manors of Björneborg and Koivisto, the fisheries of the Kumo River, the sawmill of Norrmark and the Loima mill at Vittis, among other locations.

As in all parts of Finland, rent remained continually unpaid in the county, particularly in years of crop failure. In 1664 arrears to the amount of 6,646 were cancelled, and 5,136 dalers worth of arrears remained to be collected. According to a list of payments in arrears drawn up in 1665 by the bailiff Påhl Påhlsson Callia, the peasants of the county were in arrears in rent to the amount of 7,265 silver dalers. The oldest arrears dated from the founding of the county. Callia's lists were full of caustic comments and suggestions regarding the peasants in arrears:

"... has no concern about paying his rent or arrears, more suitable as a soldier", "penniless and a great scoundrel, has no concern for his payments and conceals his yield", "drinks as long as he can and as long as there is beer in the locality", "it would be better for someone else to be given the farm", "must pay his arrears or lose his hereditary rights". The image of the prevalence of unwillingness to pay rent in comparison with inability to do so cannot be believed as such, but in any case it seems probable that some of the peasants in arrears were deliberately disobedient.[100]

In practice, however, Callia could carry out his threats only with regard to the worst recalcitrants. According to the accounts and cadastres of the county, only a few peasants lost their hereditary rights on account of arrears and were evicted from their holdings; a couple of them were marked as vagrants in

---

99   Jokipii, *Suomen kreivi- ja vapaaherrakunnat*, I, pp. 284–285, 289.

100   RA, Bielkesamlingen, Gustav Horn och Sigrid Bielke, Gods- och länshandlingar, Björneborgs grevskap och Vampula gård, Restlängd 1664, 1665 & 1669, E 2424–2425 (vols 28–29, KA, FR 200); Bielkesamlingen, Nils Bielke och Eva Horn, Godshandlingar, Björneborgs grevskap, Jordebok 1679, E 2160 (vol. 21, KA, FR 196). Appointed crown bailiff of Lower Satakunta in 1688, Callia did not recognize so-called hopeless arrears that were to be left uncollected – his list of arrears mentions mainly the alternatives "paid" or "must pay"/"must be collected". KA, 7383 b (verification book 1689), pp. 6684–6906.

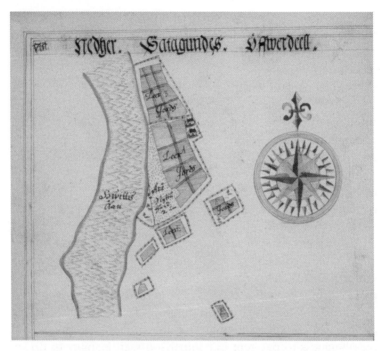

Through their numerous complaints, Sigfred and his son Henrik of Hellilä village in the parish of Vittis caused major pains to Påhl Påhlsson Callia, the bailiff of the County of Björneborg in the 1670s. The picture shows a land survey map drawn by Jonas Streng over Hellilä in 1646. Archives of the National Land Survey Authority / National Archives of Finland.

connection with conscription, but they were not taken as soldiers. Conscription was at least a means of pressuring them into hiring a substitute – a means of both economic and emotional pressure. The crown lists of arrears, however, show that also a few other peasants in arrears to the county were in fact evicted and some were even conscripted. It was easy to evict peasants who had lost their hereditary rights as long as there was a suitable excuse (e.g. arrears). In many cases, these matters were taken to court only when the eviction was disputed. Some of the evicted peasants and their families had to go begging, and one of them, Henrik Grelsson of Jalanoja in Vittis, starved to death.[101]

In the early 1670s Callia found himself in serious difficulties when a number of evicted peasants of Vittis began to complain about him to Countess Sigrid Bielke, the Åbo Court of Appeal and to Stockholm to the highest officials of the realm. Even Callia's brother, Crown Bailiff Henrik Påhlsson Callia supported the plaintiffs by claiming that his brother had collected too much rent from them without giving a receipt. The conflict between the brothers was partly due to the county's tax arrears to the crown. In general terms, this was a question of a struggle for hegemony between the crown and the county. Påhl Påhlson was hard put to make the countess believe him and not the plaintiffs. In his letters he underlined the fact if the plaintiffs were not made to take responsibility for their arrears, for example by taking punishment by running a gauntlet if they had no funds, the other peasants would cease to pay their rent and no one would dare any more to repossess the holding of an evictee. Callia crushed the plaintiffs with the aid of the favourable rulings of the district court sessions and the *lagman* court. The plaintiffs were reduced to the status of penniless vagabonds.[102] This restoration of

---

[101] See previous and following note. Crown list of arrears: KA, 7336, pp. 2502–2508, 2531–2535 (Ulvsby, Kumo, Vittis). On evicitions, see also KA, judicial district of Vemo and Lower Satakunta I, judgment book 1674, pp. 198–199/78, Lower Satakunta II, judgment book 1684, p. 717, 1685, p. 747 (Kumo autumn district court sessions 17.–18.12.1674 and Vemo autumn and winter district court sessions 13.–14.10.1684 and 23.–24.1.1685). On the eviction of tenant farmer on donated land, see Anders Thoré, *Akademibondens plikt, universitetets rätt: Feodala produktionsförhållanden vid Uppsala universitets gods 1650–1790* (Uppsala, 2001), pp. 58–78; Jutikkala, *Bonden i Finland genom tiderna*, pp. 157, 165, 173–174; Jutikkala, 'Väestö ja yhteiskunta,' pp. 311–314.

[102] RA, Bielkesamlingen, Gustav Horn och Sigrid Bielke, Brev från underhavande på finska gods, P. Påhlsson to S. Bielke 21.12.1673 – 13.5.1675 and appendices , E 2385, P. Påhlsson to book-keeper J. Gernman 28.11.1673 – 18.6.1675 and appendices, E 2386 (vols 11–12, KA, FR 197–198); Jokipii, *Porin kreivikunta*, pp. 162–166; Haikari, *Suurläänitys – perintötilallisen uhka?*, pp. 34–90 (According to Haikari, the county put pressure on the peasants in arrears by putting on sale their hereditary rights at district court sessions; it was only in the hopeless cases that it purchased the rights for itself). The countess suggested that the evictees Sigfred and Henrik of Hellilä were to pay off

81

discipline was no longer interaction but repression.

Here too the peasants (or those among them who rebelled – insubordination was not as widespread in the large County of Björneborg as it appeared to be in the domain of Bjärnå manor) regarded the bailiff to be their tormentor and sought restitution from the countess and the Åbo Court of Appeal, which, unlike the local courts, was not under the control of the county.

The crop failure of 1675 led the poor of Vittis to take matters in their own hands and to steal grain from where it could be found. A few enlisted men formed a band of thieves threatening others with violence and the burning of a village. The extraordinary district court sessions at Vittis dealt with some twenty accused members of the group, sentencing one to death and the rest to fines and other forms of punishment. Some of the members of the band were not caught, and it even included women. It is hard to say whether all those involved acted in concert. The band of thieves does not necessarily have to be regarded as a protest against the county, but the crop failure and its repercussions tested social stability.[103]

In no way did Påhl Påhlsson Callia and Hans Hansson Gode, inspector of the county, close their eyes to the plight of the peasants as a result of crop failure. They repeatedly requested Gustav Horn and Sigrid Bielke to give the peasants seed and to give concessions with regard to rent and arrears,[104] and this was often done. Undue inflexibility would only have ruined the

---

their arrears with work, but Callia maintained that the work of the "Hellilä scoundrels" was not even worth their keep, in other works these men of Vittis – to quote a Finnish proverb – ate more than they earned (E 2385, P. Påhlsson to S. Bielke 3.3.1675). On restoration of discipline, see also KA, judicial district of Vemo and Lower Satakunta I, judgment book 1656, pp. 342–345, 1674, p. 8 (Vittis autumn district court sessions 20.–22.11.1656 and Vittis winter district court sessions 20.–21.1.1674).

[103] RA, Bielkesamlingen, P. Påhlsson to J. Gernman 6.12.1675 with appendices (on the band of thieves), on individual cases of thieving: 18.12.1674 & P. Påhlsson to S. Bielke 6.4.1675, E 2386 & 2385.

[104] E.g. RA, Wijksamlingen, Gustav Horn och Sigrid Bielke, H. Hansson to G. Horn 5.4.1652, E 2820 (vol. 82, KA, FR 221); RA, Bielkesamlingen, P. Påhlsson to S. Bielke 3.3.1675, E 2385 (vol. 11, KA, FR 197–198).

Thief. Drawing in the legal part of the medieval manuscript *Codex Aboensis*, early 15th century. Helsinki University Library.

peasants, whereby they would not have provided even the small amounts that could be obtained through concessions. But there were hardly any longer-term reductions of rent (*förmedlingar*) in the county (except at the very end of the donation period), which led to an accumulation of large sums in arrears, particularly in the parish of Vittis, which, unlike Ulvsby, had only a small number of abandoned farms exempted from tax or rent because of inability to pay taxes or because of being uninhabited.[105] In this respect

[105] RA, Bielkesamlingen, Räkenskaper & jordeböcker 1660–1674, Restlängd 1664, 1665 & 1669, E 2424–2425 (vols 28–29, KA, FR 200); RA, Bielkesamlingen, Nils Bielke och Eva Horn, Godshandlingar, Björneborgs grevskap, E 2160 (vol. 21, KA, FR 196).

measures and related policy were less flexible than for example in Bjärnå, or on crown land.

The County of Björneborg produced between three and five thousand silver dalers per annum.[106] Since this yield (i.e. rent from the peasants and the yield from the agriculture, livestock and fisheries of the manors after deduction of costs[107]) was nonetheless good, there was ultimately little need for concern over the accumulation of arrears, especially since it was impossible to fundamentally rectify this problem. Both Bjärnå manor and the County of Björneborg were a continuous source of affluence for their owners. All resources that could in any way be spared were sent to Sweden for their use. The same course was followed by the owners of Kumogård manor and without doubt by almost all members of the nobility living in Sweden.

The county had continually strained relations with the crown. They competed over the limited resources of the peasants, which were insufficient for the taxes and rent demanded by both.[108] In the 1670s, when the county was unable to forward its taxes to the crown as a result of crop failures and the continuous transfer of resources to Stockholm, Governor Harald Oxe of the Province of Åbo and Björneborg threatened Påhl Påhlsson Callia with imprisonment, and even the death sentence. In other words the bailiff was treated no better than a common vagrant. The threat of the one-quarter restitution in the form of relinquishing holdings hung over the county, and was carried out.[109] In this situation Callia, and many other bailiffs of the donated lands, had to take the aims and needs of the peasants into account more than they wanted to in their hearts. Callia's lists of arrears describe his real views of the peasants. In practice, he had enough problems with

---

[106] Jokipii, 'Porin kreivikunta,' p. 141.
[107] In the accounts of the donated lands the former were usually entered into the tenant-farmer accounts and the latter into the accounts of the main manor.
[108] RA, Wijksamlingen, H. Hansson to G. Horn 10.1. & 8.3.1652, E 2820 (vol. 82, KA, FR 221); Jokipii, 'Porin kreivikunta,' pp. 156–159.
[109] RA, Bielkesamlingen, P. P. Påhlsson to J. Gernman 16.3.1674 and appendices, 26.3.1674, 18.2. & 15.3.1676, E 2386 (vol. 12, KA, FR 198); Jokipii, 'Porin kreivikunta', p. 108.

the worst recalcitrants. He banished them and individual peasants in arrears who had become eyesores to him, but he had to leave the rest of defaulters alone.

INFLAMED RELATIONS AT KUMOGÅRD MANOR

General Arvid Forbus, of a Finnish family of Scots extraction, was given the title of baron in 1652 and the office of privy councillor the next year. In the late 1640s he began to stake out for himself the crown manor of Kumogård and its lands, establishing them as his donations in 1650–1651. After adding new donations to his former donated properties in the 1660s, Forbus had approximately 50 *mantal* units in the parish of Kumo in 1664. These were mostly donations as defined in the Norrköping resolution. Forbus is given here as an example of a nobleman, who unlike other members of the high nobility mentioned above, did not even pretend to be a fair and reasonable master to his peasants. Instead, he sought to extract the maximum benefits from them within the bounds of the law and administrative procedures, with no regard for consequences.

On his donated lands in various parts of Finland Forbus tried to make the peasants agree to contractual rent instead of the rent laid down in the crown cadastre with a raising of the day-labour requirements. The disputes relating to day labour, mounted service and the amassing of hereditary rights caused by him in the parish of Nyby are discussed below. The events at Nyby are well-known. Forbus, however, immediately met with opposition also among the peasants of Kumogård manor. Already in 1648, bailiff Henrik Jöransson informed Forbus that the tenants of Ylistaro village in Kumo refused to carry out the labour day per week that was required of them. With the aid of junker Jöran Horn, the bailiff sent the leader of the recalcitrants to military service in Livonia, and another insubordinate person was sent to join him.

Governor Lorentz Creutz the Elder of the Province of Åbo and Björneborg often served as a mediator for the crown and the

85

nobility in cases involving insubordination by the peasants. In the summer of 1649 Creutz arrived at Kumo and assembled the local peasants. The most obstinate ones among them fled into the woods, but the governor had a few of them apprehended and thrown into the manor jail. As a result, the peasants agreed to provide two weekly labour days. One of the peasants had struck Henrik Jöransson, but could not be brought before the court as he had drowned. In their correspondence, Creutz referred to Forbus as "my dear brother" and he guarded the landed interests of the latter, who resided outside Finland.

The peasants now complained to Per Brahe, governor-general of Finland, of the day-labour requirements, which they felt were unreasonable. Brahe ordered Creutz to act as an arbitrator in this matter. An agreement was drawn up on February 18, 1651, which specifically concerned tax peasants still in possession of their hereditary rights. The crown did not give any support to those who had lost these rights, who had to agree with their landlord themselves on day-labour services as best they could. According to the agreement, the tax peasants were free to pay their rent according to the crown cadastre and were not bound by the contractual rent laid down by Forbus. As they had previously provided day labour for the crown manors they now had to give Forbus one day per week, except in the hay-cutting season when only two days per three weeks were required.[110]

The tax peasants of Kumogård manor, however, paid rent according to the crown cadastre for only a period of two years, after which they were persuaded or pressured into paying the same kind of contractual rent as their non-hereditary fellow peasants. The manor kept no records whatsoever of day labour at the time, but the day-labour requirements of those (i.e. the tax peasants) who now adopted the contractual rent presumably

---

110 LUB, De la Gardieska arkivet, Topographica, Kumo, Forsby, Ånäs, vol. 44, H. Jöransson to A. Forbus 19.10.1648, 7.1.1650 & 24.5.1652, vol. 35, agreement drawn up by L. Creutz 18.2.1651, Creutz to Forbus 5.10.1650 (KA, FR 776, 772).

Kumogård manor was founded in the 14th century on the banks of the River Kumo. The parish bears the same name as the river which was a channel of trading and communication between the sea and the inland. The rapids provided fine fishing sites and the banks were excellent lands for cultivation. No wonder that the place caught the eye of General Arvid Forbus. His son-in-law and successor as the owner of the manor was Axel Julius De la Gardie, younger brother of Magnus Gabriel De la Gardie. This drawing of the manor house by land surveyor Olof Mörk dates back to the year 1690 and does not portray the actual appearance of Kumogård; the white two-storey building was the regular symbol of a manor in a land survey map. The manor and the adjacent buildings were destroyed in a fire on 28 April 1691. Archives of the National Land Survey Authority / National Archives of Finland.

remained the same as laid down in 1651. This was no great compensation as the contractual rent of the tax peasants was now clearly higher than those laid down in the crown cadastre. Without doubt they thus had to compensate Forbus for the smaller amount of day labour. Raising the rent was of course contrary to the agreement negotiated by Governor Creutz in 1651. The agreement appears to have been only a temporary solution for Forbus to pacify the peasants and buy time until it was again possible to raise the burden of also the tax peasants.

The contractual rent of the peasants who had lost their hereditary rights was equal to or at lower level than the rent laid down in the crown cadastre. They compensated for this seemingly lenient treatment by labour services for Forbus. Following the established custom, many of the peasants tended the inventory livestock of the manor.[111]

But even these changes to the position of the tax peasants were not enough for Forbus and the manor. According to the 1665 cadastre, in which the day-labour services were exceptionally recorded, each farm – with only a few exceptions – provided two days of labour per week for the manor. Owing to the difficulty of identifying holdings and the taxes and rent in question it is difficult to make comparisons with earlier rent and crown taxes. Two examples, however, suggest that the tax peasants, inasmuch as they still had this status, were not given reductions in rent in compensation for their doubled day-labour services.[112]

Forbus naturally did his utmost to benefit from his donated properties, but even at Kumogård it was necessary in 1657–1658, when the bailiff was changed, to annul a great amount of rent in arrears owed by the peasants.[113] The raising of the rent did not

[111] Vols 36–37, Jordebok 1651–1653 (KA, FR 772–773); KA, 7294 (cadastre 1665).
[112] Vol. 38, Jordebok 1664–1665, vol. 39, Räkning 1674 (KA, FR 773–774). The contractual rent changed somewhat over the years. The collection includes different cadastres, but of primary interest are the ones according to which the peasants' rent produce was collected and not the ones drawn up for the needs of crown taxation.
[113] Vol. 37 (KA, FR 773).

produce the desired benefit except perhaps in terms of increased day labour. These benefits were offset by permanently inflamed relations between the manor and the peasants. Later, in connection with the major changes that took place at the end of the 17th century, when the peasants dared to avoid providing day labour, the only benefits of the manor's explicit policy of exploitation were lost. It was thus no wonder that for example at Bjärnå manor it was only tested how much the peasants would agree to diminish their conditions, and when there was stubborn opposition the equilibrium of crown cadastre and established practice, the unofficial social contract, was again adopted.

Arvid Forbus died in 1665 and Kumogård manor was inherited by his daughter Sofia Juliana Forbus and her husband Count Axel Julius De la Gardie[114]. In the restitution of donated properties in 1683 the manor was restored to the crown, but at the end of the same year King Charles XI let Sofia keep Kumogård, because her father had paid for its allodial rights; part of the lands of the manor remained in Sofia's possession solely as her donated property for her lifetime. De la Gardie and his spouse had to provide cavalrymen from Kumogård and the properties left in connection with it.

The manor's indefinite and uncertain situation as a result of the restitution and long after 1683 again goaded the peasants to reluctance with regard to day-labour services. They now preferred to regard themselves as subjects of the crown, and the day labour demanded by Forbus and De la Gardie no longer applied to them. The crown demanded extraordinary taxes even from the boundary peasants from whom the manor had not demanded them – the latter no doubt in order to extort instead more labour from them. This compounded the reluctance of the peasants, for they thought that the extraordinary taxes would readily compensate the day labour. The crown bailiff would from time to time inform the peasants that they did not have to provide day-labour services for the manor.

---

[114]   Privy councillor 1674, governor-general of Estonia 1687.

Already in March 1684 the district court sessions at Kumo dealt with the refusal of peasants to carry out their day-labour obligations. They had not provided day labour despite the orders of the Åbo Court of Appeal regarding the division of day-labour services between the lessee now on his way out and the manor. Crown documents were read to the peasants at the court sessions demonstrating that the rights of the former owners had been partly restored.

The manor had levied such taxes from the peasants which the crown now regarded as belonging to it. As Sofia Forbus and her spouse continually demanded the bailiff to forward the resources produced by the manor to Sweden, the manor was unable to pay all its taxes to the crown, as a result of which the crown bailiff threatened to confiscate chattels or even the whole manor. Relations with the crown became strained in exactly the same way as in the County of Björneborg in the 1670s.

In 1684 Count De la Gardie issued instructions to bailiff Henrik Strandsten. The purpose of this was to make the manor benefit its owners as much as possible despite all the unfavourable changes that had taken place. Among other things, the instructions ordered the bailiff not to permit the peasants to do all their two contractual days of work per week but to save labour days for the best harvest time. The tenants had to pay for their arrears by participating in construction work for the manor. Insubordination was punished by a few days on bread and water in the manor jail. The arrears of the recalcitrants were to be expropriated if necessary by reaping their harvests, but they had to be helped nonetheless with grain for bread and seed.

The amount of weekly day labour had thus doubled compared with the agreement of 1651, but the latter agreement had only concerned the hereditary tax peasants, and by the 1660s at the latest even they had been forced to provide two labour days a week. The ones who had lost their hereditary rights had no doubt always had to carry out these day-labour services that were no doubt standard practice in many manors. Insofar as the history of the parish from 1860 is reliable, the majority of the peasants of

Kumo Parish had lost their hereditary rights in the years 1648–1683. It is not known whether or not the manor systematically obtained them.

In 1688 the manor had to grant the peasants the choice of keeping to the contractual rent and its day-labour services or following the crown cadastre's arrangement of fewer labour days while paying the rent precisely in the items and produce listed in the crown cadastre. This condition was meant to make the latter alternative a more difficult choice, but many of the peasants nonetheless chose it. In the contractual rent two labour days per week remained in use in the summer, but one of the two days was abolished for the winter season because the crown had levied extraordinary taxes on the peasants. The choices of the peasants were ratified in district court sessions. They reminded them of the partly uncompleted day-labour services of the past two years, which now had to be carried out.

Throughout the process Strandsten complained about the reluctance of the peasants. One of them, Henrik Jakobsson Kuitti would go about drunk with an axe and a knife, threatening the inhabitants of the manor that no one in power could chase him off his land. But Kuitti did not pay even a quarter of his rent and labour services. The others were hardly any more conscientious. Strandsten took the peasants to court over fishing waters which the peasants first seized from the manor but were finally reinstated by the bailiff through the ruling of the district court sessions. Another peasant was fined in the 1686 court sessions for resisting confiscation of arrears and baring his knife. In the following year, Strandsten boasted of having confiscated 150 barrels of grain from the peasants.[115]

[115] KA, judicial district of Lower Satakunta II, judgment book 1684, p. 530, Vemo and Lower Satakunta II, judgment book 1694, p. 68 (Kumo winter district court sessions 1.–4.3.1684 and 16.–17.3.1694 (The peasants still went to court against the manor over rapids rights as later as 1694); LUB, De la Gardieska arkivet, Kumo, Forsby, Ånäs, vol. 34, N. Lietzens memorial 20.10.1686, A. J. De la Gardie to L. Creutz 21.12.1686, Kumo, Extraordinarie härads ting 16.2.1688, vol. 45, S. Rusk to H. Strandsten 18.3.1683, Strandsten to his employers 1.& 18.10.& 8.12.1685, 22.3., 15.5., 15.6., 12.8.& 20.11.1686,

The relations between Kumogård manor and its peasants were quite strained. But this was at most a question of insubordination; to speak of rebellion and insurgency would be an exaggeration.

In 1688 De la Gardie and his wife had their fill of Strandsten, who was proven to have lined his own pockets with rent from the peasants. Strandsten was taken in shackles to Åbo Castle to be interrogated.[116]

The new bailiff, Johan Asmundsson, in turn had to resign in 1693/1694. The owners of the manor maintained that he had let the peasants in the worst conditions provide mounted service while allowing those better off to be the tenants of the crown. De la Gardie refused to grant the remission proposed by the peasants and suspected that if the crops had failed it was the result of mismanagement and not the weather. De la Gardie and Sofia Forbus maintained that the bailiff had sided with the peasants, which may be true, since Johan Asmundsson did not complain about their insubordination in the manner of his predecessor.[117]

Governor Lorentz Creutz the Younger had branded Strandsten to be a useless man who was never sober,[118] but the De la Gardies reinstated him. Creutz was not as closely connected to this generation of owners as his father, of the same name, had been with Sofia's father. In 1694, the peasants who had farmed Kumogård manor on a sharecropping arrangement since 1692 were ordered by De la Gardie to begin to pay a higher contractual

11.1.1687 with appendices, 10.3., 28.5. & 1.10.1687, 16.2., 28.2., 23.3. & 12.6.1688, count/countess to Strandsten 26.12.1684 & 12.1.1686 (on deliveries to Sweden passim), instructions to Strandsten 3.10.1684, Kumo, Ordinarie häradsvinterting 8.–11.2.1686, vol. 46, instructions to J. Asmundsson 30.5.1688 (KA, FR 771, 776); Lindström, 'Kumo Socken uti historiskt hänseende,' pp. 244–246 (Kumogård in the 17th c.), 276 .

116 Vol. 45, H. Strandsten to A. J. De la Gardie 30.4. & 11.8.1688, Rannsakning 1685, S. J. Forbus to Strandsten 20.9.1687 and other correspondence on the dismissal of the bailiff in the same collection (KA, FR 776).

117 Vol. 34, S. J. Forbus to O. Edner 6.12.1692, vol. 35, A. J. De la Gardie to J. Asmundsson 10.10.1693, vol. 46, Asmundsson to De la Gardie 28.8.1693, L. Creutz to Forbus 19.12.1693, vol. 48, Uppsats vad Kumo säteri importerat 1688–1692 (KA, FR 772, 777–778).

118 Vol. 34, L. Creutz to S. J. Forbus 27.11.1694 (KA, FR 772).

rent than laid down in the original arrangement or leave.[119] Strandsten immediately began his old complaints about the resistance of the peasants, to which he claimed the former bailiff had goaded them. It was Strandsten who urged the count and countess to alter the contract with the tenant farmers and to get rid of the former ones. Already in 1695 Strandsten required the assistance of the governor and the crown bailiff to make the peasants fulfill their obligations.[120]

Noblemen residing outside Finland often found it difficult to find an honest and able bailiff or overseer for their lands, because many of these subordinates used their position to gain as many benefits as possible from both the peasants and the owners. In addition to Strandsten and Asmundsson we should also remember Wrangel's bailiff Per Skarp and Petter Hackes who was bailiff at Bjärnå from 1671 to 1674 and who died in drunkenness. Hackes and his widow did their utmost to obtain additional benefits from his master on the basis of crop failure.[121] The interests of the noblemen and their bailiffs by no means converged at all times. A good landlord regarded it as his duty to protect his peasants against malfeasance on the part of the bailiffs, which was also in the landlord's economic and "political" interest. The latter implied avoiding disputes that could be avoided. The peasants sensed this conflict of interest well when complaining about the severity of the bailiff to the noble owners. The tenant farmers of Kumogård manor, however, understood correctly that they could not expect any improvements to their treatment from Forbus and his daughter or Axel Julius De la Gardie.[122]

---

[119] Vol. 35, instructions to H. Strandsten 14.11.1694 (KA, FR 772).

[120] Vol. 45, H. Strandsten to his employers 27.4. & 4.6.1694, L. Creutz to the crown bailiff 17.8.1695 (KA, FR 776).

[121] RA, Rydboholmssamlingen, Wrangelska godshandlingar, Bjärnå, the accounts of P. Hackes and his widow 1671–1675, E 8016, C. G. Wrangels ekonomiska brevväxling, Hackes to Wrangel s.d., E 7942 (vols 550, 476, KA, FR 217, 215); Litzen, *Perniön historia*, I, p. 249.

[122] Arvid Forbus, however, would sometimes alleviate the position of a peasant who had lost his property in a fire, and De la Gardie forgave arrears.

The next example of the cold-hearted economic management pursued by the Forbus and De la Gardie families came in the severe winter of famine and mortality in 1695–1696[123], when the count and countess blankly refused to listen to and believe Strandsten's report that hardly anything could be expected from the peasants, because they were dying of hunger. In an unsigned draft letter to the bailiff written by the count or countess in Stockholm on May 12, 1696, at a time of famine and high mortality which could not have passed unnoticed even in the capital, the bailiff is criticized for not following the agreement drawn up in 1694 between the tenant farmers of Kumogård and the provincial governor requiring the former to supply 100 barrels of grain per annum regardless of crop failure. In closing the author of the letter sarcastically asks Strandsten whether the crop failure also applied to butter, frieze and slaughter animals, which the peasants were contractually obliged to send to their masters in Sweden. The occasional desire to purge subordinates that had been displayed by the count and countess now threatened Strandsten for a second time, but he avoided the shackles and the dungeons of Åbo Castle by dying in May 1696.[124]

LIFE UNDER THE RULE OF THE NOBLES

On March 4, 1684, King Charles XI of Sweden issued conscription instructions to the governors and military authorities of the provinces of Åbo and Björneborg, Nyland and Tavastehus,

---

[123] Mortality, however, did not peak until the spring of 1697. See Muroma, *Suurten kuolovuosien (1696–1697) väestönmenetys Suomessa*; Oiva Turpeinen, 'Suomen väestö 1638–1815 sekä vertailu Viroon,' *Ihmisiä, ilmiöitä ja rakenteita historian virrassa*, Professori Antero Heikkiselle 60-vuotispäivänä omistettu juhlakirja (Joensuu, 2001), pp. 14–26, 29–32, 43, 48.

[124] LUB, above-mentioned collection, vol. 45, H. Strandsten to S. Forbus 29.9.1695 and to the book-keeper 16.2.1696, S. Forbus to H. Kluwensich 16.12.1695, A. J. De la Gardie to L. Creutz 7.4.1696, Forbus or De la Gardie to Strandsten 28.4. & 12.5.1696 (KA, FR 776).

Ostrobothnia, Närke and Värmland, according to which it would not be permissible for nobles to continually order the same appended holding to place a soldier in the service of the crown, thereby seeking the ruination of the farm and its hereditary rights.[125] Such measures were actually taken in the 1640s at Asikkala in Tavastia,[126] by a nobleman Matts Creutzhammar who also sought in other ways to extort additional benefits from his peasants. The authority of the noble master to choose from among his subordinates a suitable man for military service was on the whole an excellent method of maintaining discipline.[127]

In Västergötland, Södermanland and Uppland in Sweden and in the Barony of Kimito, the parish of Esbo and the County of Björneborg in Finland the acquisition of hereditary rights from peasants in arrears was not the result of any systematic policies. Such transfers nevertheless took place, sometimes to a considerable degree. The nobleman would acquire the hereditary rights to a holding when it he could see that nothing else could be obtained any more from a peasant hopelessly in debt (at Kimito and Esbo) or had the rights reannounced in district court sessions to be on sale, thus forcing the peasant to pay his arrears (County of Björneborg). Upon seizing the hereditary rights, the nobleman would lose the arrears of the peasant, who would now be put off the land. In some cases the peasant would voluntarily sell his hereditary rights – through ignorance or because of having no other alternative.

The nobleman would benefit from owning hereditary rights when rearranging his property (for example when establishing a *säter* manor providing additional exemptions from taxes), because a peasant lacking hereditary rights could easily be removed from his land. It was also possible to demand more day-labour services from peasant without hereditary rights than was decreed by the

---

[125]   KA, 6828, p. 56 (also the register of Charles XI on the same date).
[126]   Heikki Ylikangas, *Aikansa rikos – historiallisen kehityksen valaisijana* (Juva, 2000), pp. 141–145.
[127]   Jutikkala, 'Väestö ja yhteiskunta,' pp. 294–295, 313, 315–316.

35. Forbus.

Frih. 1652. Introd 1652. † 1665.

Queen Christina promoted General Arvid Forbus (1598–1665) to the rank of baron in 1652. Kumo was only his nominal barony, since it did not include any public authority typical of counties or baronies. In 1653 Forbus became a privy councillor. National Board of Antiquities.

Riksdag for tax peasants, but on some large properties as in the County of Björneborg the existing amount of day labour was sufficient. In some areas a cautious policy was followed, while in other parts of the country – particularly on Southeast Finland (Southeast Tavastia, East Nyland and the present-day Kymmenedalen region) – both Baltic and local noblemen ruthlessly acquired the hereditary rights of their appended peasants.[128]

At Artsjö and elsewhere in the administrative parish of Nyby and in other parts of Southeast Tavastia, the peasants who provided cavalrymen for crown service were a nuisance to the above-mentioned Baron Arvid Forbus, because mounted service exempted them from most taxes (and corresponding rent). For the crown, cavalry service was more important than the interests of an individual nobleman. Accordingly, in 1640 the regency of the realm forbade Forbus from evicting peasants providing cavalry service and enjoying hereditary rights. A peasant providing cavalry service who had lost his hereditary rights could be moved to an equal holding given to him in compensation by Forbus, but the cavalry service had to continue as before.

With the aid of various tricks, however, and the support of high crown officials in Finland, Forbus managed to make his cavalry-service peasants give up this duty and to obtain their hereditary rights, whereupon there were no obstacles to raising rent or to rearranging the properties. In 1663 Baron Lorentz Creutz the Elder, Forbus's friend, who was often used as a mediator by the crown and the nobility and who had left the post of governor of the Province of Åbo and Björneborg and had been appointed privy councillor in 1660, persuaded three peasants of Nyby Parish (in Kuivanto in Orimattila) to give up cavalry service for the crown. Creutz described Forbus's other cavalry-service peasants as "rebels" and claimed that the Sultan of Turkey and the Holy Roman Emperor would sooner come to terms than these peasants would give up cavalry service. The peasants knew that if they gave in, their master could gradually bring them under complete

---

[128] Ernby, *Adeln och bondejorden*, passim; Ågren, *Adelns bönder och kronans*, pp. 178–194; Revera, *Gods och gård 1650–1680*, passim; Gardberg, *Kimito friherreskap*, pp. 104–106; August Ramsay, *Esbo II: Esbo socken och Esbogård på 1600-talet* (Helsingfors, 1936), pp. 54–56; Jutikkala, *Bonden i Finland genom tiderna*, pp. 166–176; Ylikangas, *Aikansa rikos*, pp. 307–311; Katajala, *Suomalainen kapina*, p. 261 and passim. On the County of Björneborg above.

subordination, regardless of pacifying assurances made to them by the high-ranking representatives of the crown. In 1663, Forbus and Creutz pressured (with no results) the Swedish regency to make a decision whereby noblemen were less impeded to transfer with exchange of land unprofitable cavalry-service peasants from their *säter* manor. At the same time, the regency increased the amount of land donated to Forbus, which means that Forbus and Creutz arranged matters at the highest possible level, for the benefit of the former and the loss of the cavalry-service peasants.

Forbus systematically arranged for himself the hereditary rights of whole villages as the result of arrears. He drew up rent agreements with his peasants that provided him with new benefits and took no note of whether they still had their hereditary rights. In 1651, however, the district court sessions of Nyby exempted the peasants who had kept their hereditary rights from the two weekly labour days to which they had agreed by contract. The court maintained that the ruling of the Swedish *Riksdag* concerning the day-labour services of tax peasants annulled the agreement made with Forbus.

Forbus treated his peasants poorly and he was in continuous conflict with them. For example, at Christmastime in 1650 the peasants of Nyby ceased to provide labour days for Forbus. This was a time of unrest in the realm; in the *Riksdag* sessions held in connection with the coronation of Queen Christina the non-noble estates worked politically against the nobility and the *Riksdag* began to lay down and restrict day-labour services; unrest spread from the *Riksdag* further into society at large. In May-June 1651, the administration of the Province of Nyland and Tavastehus and Governor Erik Andersson Oxe himself ordered the reluctant peasants of Nyby, upon pain of eviction, to carry out the normal day-labour services decreed by the *Riksdag* according to whether they still had hereditary rights to their land.[129]

---

[129] Jutikkala, 'Väestö ja yhteiskunta,' pp. 292–297, 301, 303, 318–319, 332; Ylikangas, *Aikan-sa rikos*, pp. 307–311; LUB, De la Gardieska arkivet, Kumo, Forsby, Ånäs, vol. 34, resolutions of the provincial government and governor of the Province of Nyland and Tavastehus 28.5.1651 and 29.6.1651, vol. 35, L. Creutz to A. Forbus 12.9. & 7.11.1663, E. J. Creutz

In his history of Tavastia, Eino Jutikkala notes that "hereditary rights quietly and steadily flowed into the hands of the nobility." But, with the exception of Baltic nobles, few among the aristocracy of Tavastia consistently amassed the hereditary rights of peasants. The crown also seized hereditary rights as the result of unpaid taxes.[130]

Count Arvid Wittenberg[131], who was in possession of the Barony of Loimijoki, or in practice his local representatives, obtained the hereditary rights to a number of holdings through barter, monetary compensation and by annulling arrears. Wittenberg thus marked out for himself not only manorial lands and mill rapids sites at Loimijoki but also a position at the Kauttua rapids in Eura. Unlike Forbus's transactions, these changes were not the subject of any complaints, which means that there was little coercion involved in the actions of Wittenberg or his representatives.[132] In the judicial district (*domsaga*) of Vemo and Lower Satakunta, the hereditary rights of holdings were officially announced as available at district court sessions from time to time (they had to be declared three times to be available for purchase by relatives, who had right of pre-emption; also the crown and on tax-exempted land nobles took precedence before possible buyers outside the family) and

---

to Forbus 14.5.1662 and the agreement drawn up by H. Horn and L. Creutz 18.10.1663 (KA, FR 771–772). In 1651 Forbus's bailiff Erik Israelsson claimed of course that the donated-land peasants of Nyby did not have hereditary rights. Governor Oxe reminded the peasants of a royal letter from 1574 in which 12 annual labour days to the crown were decreed for the inhabitants of the district of Borgå, in addition to auxiliary labour days. Please note that I have not dealt with the material of Artsjö and Jackarby manors in the same collection. Artsjö manor would certainly be worth a broader study, because there was still unrest in the locality at the beginning of the following century. Kujala, *Miekka ei laske leikkiä*, pp. 187–188; *De la Gardiska Archivet*, 13 (Lund, 1840), pp. 105–108.

[130] Jutikkala, 'Väestö ja yhteiskunta,' pp. 280–333 (day labour 290–299, evictions in connection with the founding of *säter* estates 274–276).

[131] Privy councillor 1651, count 1652, military commander in the Thirty Years' War, died as a prisoner of war in Poland in 1657.

[132] KA, judicial district of Lower Satakunta I, judgment book 1652, p. 387, Vemo and Lower Satakunta I, judgment book 1653, p. 66, 1654, p. 194, 1655, p. 60, 1657, p. 484 (Eura district court sessions 26.–27.5.1653, 31.1.–1.2.1654, 12.–14.6.1655, Loimijoki district court sessions 23.–24.4.1652, 9.–11.5.1657).

hereditary rights were thus obtained by noblemen,[133] but with the exception of Wittenberg no one here appears to have amassed these rights in any consistent manner.

The owners of Degerö manor in the parish of Helsinge showed the range of action that the nobles could resort to in order to obtain hereditary rights, fishing waters and benefits in general from their peasants. This situation largely involved parvenus staking out a higher social status through behaviour that could be described as arrogance or contemptuousness. Maritime customs inspector Augustin Svanström, who was raised to the nobility and who obtained the manor as a purchased donation in 1648, and his noble-born wife and widow Anna Grönfelt employed – at least according to their accusers – coercion, all manner of harassment and damaging acts and of course rent and labour requirements in excess of the crown cadastre to achieve their objectives. Anna Grönfelt's main opponent was Brita Henriks-dotter, the widow of a helmsman, but also a few other residents of Degerö claimed to have suffered injustice at the hands of the manor owners. A number of them gave up their case, but Brita persisted. She had to obtain the rulings confirming her position and rights as the holder of hereditary rights from Herman Fleming, governor-general of Finland (1666), the regency of the realm (1669), King Charles XI (1674), the Privy Council (1675), and the Åbo Court of Appeal, not to mention lower courts. Anna Grönfelt, however, did not agree to follow the instructions of the highest authorities of the realm, and continued to harass Brita. During her lifetime, Anna did not pay Brita the compensation of 100 silver dalers which had been ordered by the Åbo Court of Appeal in 1676.[134]

---

133   E.g. KA, judicial district of Vemo and Lower Satakunta I, judgment book 1674, pp. 84–85 (11–12) (Vemo and Lokalax winter district court sessions 20.–21.3.1674).

134   KA, Topographica II, Helsinge socken 3, 1600-talets handlingar rörande Uppby hemman i Degerö by; KA, 7985 (1665), p. 10, 7986, p. 148; Markku Kuisma, *Helsinge sockens historia*, II (Jyväskylä, 1992), pp. 176, 205–209.

The Antti farmstead from the parish of Säkylä, transferred to Seurasaari open-air museum in Helsinki. Drawing by P. Hammarberg. National Board of Antiquities.

Not all members of the nobility were wealthy. In 1691 Charles XI permitted members of nobility and upper classes of poor (*miserable*) economic standing to keep their donated and enfeoffed lifetime holdings in the Province of Åbo and Björneborg. Similar properties were to be immediately restituted to the crown from others, but from the *miserables* only after their death.[135] It is obvious that at least some of these penniless noblemen did their utmost to benefit at the cost of their own peasants. It cannot be claimed, however, that such behaviour was limited to poor members of the nobility alone.

Jutikkala cites a large number of cases from Southeast Tavastia where noblemen used contracts, common in the region and ratified in district courts, to raise the amount of labour days provided by their appended peasants to two in return for a very small reduction of rent. When a nobleman established a *säter* manor on donated land at the beginning of the century, the former resident was

---

[135]   KA, Karl XI:s registratur 1691 (avskrift), to L. Creutz 30.3.1691; RA, Landshövdingars skrivelser till K.M:t, Åbo och Björneborgs län, vol. 9, L. Creutz 21.3.1691 (KA, FR 43).

101

evicted as a matter of course. A peasant could relinquish his holding only if he was not in arrears. Unpaid rent bound him to the holding in a manner that was not far removed from serfdom. If the arrears became insurmountable, the peasant could free himself of them by deserting the property. After solving his problems in this unauthorized manner, the deserter had to start life anew in another locality. Many peasants disappeared without a trace when the holding which they had received to farm from the crown or a local nobleman in return for a period of tax-exempt years again became liable to pay tax. The owners of the manors would use their right to administer corporal punishment against recalcitrants.[136]

DISPUTES IN JOCKIS, OSTROBOTHNIA AND ELIMÄ

Jesper Matsson Cruus, who had received the manor of Jockis in Southwest Tavastia as a donation in the early 17th century, made his peasants agree to contractual rent that replaced their crown taxes and exceeded their payments to a considerable degree. Nobles began to draw up rent contracts of this kind with their peasants in the early 17th century. For decades, the peasants of Jockis tried to get rid of their contractual rent and lower their payments to the same level as their neighbours, but to no avail, because the manor belonged to members of the high nobility living in Sweden (including members of the Oxenstierna family), and the province governors and judiciary of Finland readily saw matters from the perspective of the latter. The whole matter presumably arose from the fact that Cruus's contractual rent and its later adjustments (raises) differed so markedly from the crown taxes. The contracts were also put in force without conferring sufficiently with the peasants. Further problems were caused by

---

[136]   Jutikkala, 'Väestö ja yhteiskunta,' pp. 299–326.

appropriations and extraordinary taxes, which the peasants felt were covered by the contractual rent.

Unlike in the dispute at Artsjö with Forbus over the amount of contractual day labour, the district court did not release the peasants of Jockis who had preserved their hereditary rights from contractual rent. Instead, it maintained that the original contract, which had been ratified through later amendments bound them and even their descendants. The manor did not seek to obtain the hereditary rights of the peasants (Why should it have, as the contract bound them in the same way as those who had lost their family rights?) and around the middle of the century day labour was set at almost the same level as was decreed slightly later by the *Riksdag* for the tax peasants, i.e. considerably less than the two days per week that the peasants lacking hereditary rights often had to provide to their noble master. The majority of the peasants of Jockis, however, still had hereditary rights at the end of the century.

The peasants were as reluctant in paying rent as in other services and payments, which resulted in continuous court cases and related minor disturbances, of which the most serious instances were the freeing of an arrested peasant from jail, mass action and threat of violence to prevent seizure of property, and the violent prevention of the execution of office. The district courts would sometimes issue severe punishments, which, however, were enacted in more lenient form. In most cases, however, insubordinate peasants were given sizeable fines. The peasants would send their representatives to complain of how they were treated to the king and high-ranking officials in Stockholm, and to the authorities in Finland. Occasionally, the complaints were also addressed to the noblemen in possession of the donated lands. The peasants did not want to burn all bridges behind them, and balanced on the borderline of apparent loyalty and more explicit resistance.

In the restitution, Jockis manor was not restituted to the crown, but its tax peasants were freed from their contractual day-labour services. They were allowed to provide the day labour ruled by

The wooden storehouse with the clock-tower at Jockis manor, the 18th century or early 19th century. All buildings in the estate were destroyed during the Russian occupation of Finland in 1713–1721. The peasants demolished the manor house, using the logs for their own buildings. After the Treaty of Nystad, the old power and ownership structures were, however, restored and the manor was erected anew. Photo: A. Kujala.

the *Riksdag* and to pay rent in accordance with the crown cadastre, but the manor did not abide by the provincial governor's ruling and demanded contractual rent. At the close of the century, the preservation of the peasants' hereditary rights was taken up in court sessions. The case went to the Chamber College (*kammarkollegiet*) to be resolved, but was still without a verdict when Russian troops occupied Southern Finland in 1713.[137] The disputes were a source of a great deal of concern for the owner

---

137   Katajala, *Suomalainen kapina*, pp. 329–348.

of Jockis and his local representatives, and without doubt also caused economic losses through rent and day-labour services lost as the result of insubordination. It is debatable whether the raised contractual rent ultimately provided any appreciable economic benefits. The dispute had deteriorated into a matter of prestige, in which neither party wanted to give in.

In the counties and baronies of Ostrobothnia the Bothnian peasants, who were not used to the system of donated lands and were wary of it because of their own tradition of freedom, resisted interference by the nobility with local self-government and above all with their own trade in tar. The attempts of the bailiffs of the nobility to force the peasants to pay their rent in tar or ready money with the value of tax parcels calculated at higher rates than the crown values were not accepted without protest. The burghers of the Ostrobothnian towns naturally supported the peasants in their opposition to the attempts of the nobles to change the established practice of the tar trade and the payment of tax via the burghers and to appropriate the added value stemming from the export of tar from the province. The affluent and self-assertive Ostrobothnian peasant community could easily prevent the measures of the local representatives of the nobles. Resistance took place in a grey zone between apparent loyalty and more open opposition. Violence was resorted to in only a small degree on either side. The crown had its own conflicts of interest with the nobility, but even it could not refrain from reacting to insubordination, and two local peasant leaders were ruthlessly subdued. The counties and baronies of Ostrobothnia were restituted to the crown in 1675.[138]

In the donated lands of the Wrede family at Elimä in the Province of Viborg (present-day Kymmenedalen) the peasants argued with their masters throughout the 17th century. Originally from Livonia, the Wredes established their manor on the lands of the local peasants and evicted the former residents, which was by no means

---

[138]   Armas Luukko, *Etelä-Pohjanmaan historia*, III (Vaasa, 1945), pp. 586–634.

unique in the early 17th century. They forced the peasants providing mounted service into an arrangement profitable for the landlord by misinforming the authorities in Stockholm and other means. The manors expanded their property by obtaining meadows and fishing sites and by purchasing hereditary rights, the value of which the peasants did not immediately understand. Hereditary rights were also obtained on the basis of arrears. Rent was defined in agreements in which the amount of day labour was increased, because the manorial economy as a large agricultural unit required a large workforce. The day labour was compensated with an insignificant reduction of rent. With their ruthless measures, the Wredes put the local peasant community on a defensive stand and turned it against their masters in way that inflamed the situation permanently and left no way open for reconciliation.

In the district court sessions the peasants usually lost their cases, because the court maintained that the Wredes had acquired their benefits through legal sale and freedom of contract. The rulings of a court session held in 1643 were sent to Stockholm to be ratified by the regency before the local authorities dared to declare them to the averse and reluctant peasants. Through manipulation of this kind, the day-labour requirements of peasants within the freedom mile limit were raised to two days a week, double the amount of standard practice at the time. A member of the Wrede family was assistant judge of the Svea Court of Appeal, and his opinion weighed heavily in both Stockholm and in the administration and judiciary of Finland.

The court cases continued and the letter of protection issued by Queen Christina to the peasants did not provide anything beyond the security already provided by the law against despotism and arbitrariness for all and specifically against eviction for tax peasants who fulfilled their obligations. The district courts and the court of appeal noted that the Wredes had mostly acted in the manner prescribed by law. On some occasions they were fined for despotic measures. The peasants could not revoke legal agreements. The Wredes confiscated from the peasants arrears and fines for resisting the rulings of the court.

Representatives of the peasants continually visited Stockholm to lodge complaints with the authorities. On one occasion the peasants chased the manor clerk and bailiff from a disputed field with threats of violence. The dispute at Elimä aroused emotions all the way to the *Riksdag* in Stockholm. In 1651 Queen Christina ordered the Åbo Court of Appeal to pass the death sentence on the leader of the unrest and representative of the peasants in Stockholm. There was to be no clemency and the sentence was to be carried out. Nothing could make the peasants of Elimä accept the rulings dictated to them through the court and the sovereign, and the former recalcitrance and complaints continued.

At Elimä, the official decision on the restitution of donations led to a few minor incidences of violence and refusal to provide labour services. By the 1680s part of the Wrede family had not lived at Elimä for a long while. Count Fabian Wrede[139] was one of the king's favourites and he managed to save Elimä manor from restitution to the crown.

Here, the old day-labour agreements were regarded as also being binding for the tax peasants. On the other hand, most of the peasants had lost their hereditary rights by now. In 1687 a court ruling made the peasants give up their day-labour strike. The manors had suffered immense losses, which they tried to recover through confiscation from the peasants who had been on strike. Unrest continued at the manors of the other branch of the Wrede family until the Great Northern War.[140]

Katajala, on whose research the descriptions of the events that took place at Jockis and Elimä, has also studied other disputes between the peasants and nobles in possession of donated lands in the eastern parts of Nyland, Southeast Tavastia and Kymmene-dalen. They resembled the course of events at Elimä, but were generally milder and of shorter duration. The mistreatment of the

---

[139] Privy councillor 1685, President of the Chamber and Trade College and the Budget Office in 1687 etc.
[140] Katajala, *Suomalainen kapina*, pp. 220–260, 314, 318–322.

peasants has often been attributed to the German-speaking nobles who came from the Baltic lands and were used to dealing with their Estonian and Latvian peasants as serfs, who lacked the protection of the law and to whom no concessions needed to be made. According to Jutikkala, who studied conditions in Southeast Tavastia, and Katajala, it is nonetheless obvious that there were also "tormentors of the peasants" among domestic noblemen and those who had come other countries. At issue here was the founding of *säter* estates not only for increased exemption from taxes but also to practice large-scale agriculture. In such situations it became necessary to rearrange properties, to consistently obtain hereditary rights and to increase the amount of day labour.[141]

The landed property of the Baltic noble families concentrated in Southeast Finland, but they were also to be found elsewhere. Lieutenant-Colonel Friedrich von Ellert was continually involved in disputes at S:t Mårtens. It was recorded in the crown list of arrears in 1676 that Ellert had ruined one Jöran Jakobsson to the extent that arrears of two silver dalers could not be seized from him. Ellert had scraped the bottom of the barrel. Such a marking in reference to a nobleman in crown records is not unique, but nonetheless rare.[142]

The poor reputation of the Baltic nobles was also due to the fact that the peasants, and Finns and Swedes alike, usually shunned them. "Livonian Dog" was a common pejorative among the common people. In 1636 the Privy Council bluntly urged Colonel Hans Wrangel, brother of the privy councillor (and uncle of Carl Gustav Wrangel) not to treat his peasants at Pyttis in the "violent Livonian manner". Finnish courts were more timid in defending peasants against a member of the high nobility residing in Sweden than against newcomers from the Baltics.[143]

---

[141] Jutikkala, 'Väestö ja yhteiskunta,' pp. 255–328; Katajala, *Suomalainen kapina*, pp. 260–285, 315–318.
[142] KA, 7336, p. 1657; Aulis Oja, *Marttilan pitäjän historia*, I (Forssa, 1959), pp. 133, 213,
[143] Ylikangas, *Aikansa rikos*, pp. 257–261; Katajala, *Suomalainen kapina*, pp. 270–271; Jutikkala, 'Väestö ja yhteiskunta,' pp. 327–328.

RELATIONS BETWEEN THE NOBLES AND THEIR PEASANTS: CONCLUSIONS

All those who were in possession of noble estates and were able to take the guise of justice and present themselves as protectors of their peasants against unfair hirelings represented the high nobility and lived far away from their Finnish estates, in Sweden or even further away in Pomerania. This proved successful particularly at Bjärnå manor, but also in the County of Björneborg, the Barony of Kimito, Esbogård manor, several counties and baronies in Ostrobothnia and in other parts of the country. Noblemen living on their Finnish estates were not able to do this. Where disputes arose, he was necessarily the opposing part, and not an apparently outside arbitrator. The Southwest Finnish estates of the high nobility followed the same kind of authoritarian order that was legalistic while avoiding outright arbitrariness as in the large donated estates of Sweden, as described by Revera and Ågren. The role game of the well-meaning master and the loyal peasants described by Scott, and Englund in keeping with him, partly functioned quite well in Finland. It must be borne in mind that many members of the nobility had actually internalized the obligations of the good master, although they readily tested conditions through their own property administrators to see if the burden of the peasants could be increased.

It is obvious that it was worthwhile for the peasants to channel their conflicts of interest with the master into the forms of the trusting subject[144], i.e. to appeal to the benevolence of the master or at least to exert a balancing pressure in the area lying between masterly benevolence and opposition ("grey zone") rather than to resort to open opposition, which led to almost certain defeat. Their measures of securing their rights and interests were a shade stronger than the everyday resistance noted by Scott, but in principle the logic was the same. The peasants preferred the

---

[144]   Englund, *Det hotade huset*, p. 101.

Colonel, later Field Marshal and Marshal of the Realm Gustav Horn was given Esbogård manor in 1625 to serve as his benefice. In 1641 he bought the manor. The Horns were an old Finnish noble family. Gustav Horn won his merits as a military commander in the war against Poland and in the Thirty Years' War. In the battle of Nördlingen in 1634 he was defeated by the imperial troops, and he became a prisoner of war and was not released until 1642. In 1644 Horn commanded the troops that conquered the Danish provinces of Skåne and Blekinge, with the exception of the towns of Malmö and Kristianstad. In the peace treaty signed in the following year, however, these provinces remained under Danish rule. An influential man during the reign of King Charles XI, Fabian Wrede took over Esbogård in 1672, and by the year 1681 he had built the main house shown in this picture. The drawing is from 1747 by Augustin Ehrensvärd who is known as the man who had the island fortress of Sveaborg built. In his notes appended to the drawing, Ehrensvärd suggests that the owner might have intended the then fallen manor house as a habitation for owls and crows. All Finnish 17th century log-built manor houses have been destroyed. National Board of Antiquities.

smaller risk and avoided gambles. The results could remain meagre but they were nevertheless more positive than in open resistance. This was not only a question of tactics but of the fact that the peasants had largely internalized their own role as the loyal subjects of their master, thus entitled to expect him to ease their possible difficulties. This also happened: bailiffs who oppressed the peasants were dismissed and arrears were struck off the books.

In some cases the nobles simply dictated deteriorated conditions to the peasants with acceptance or resistance as their only opportunities (particularly at Elimä and Jockis; and in slightly more lenient form at Kumogård and elsewhere). These cases mainly took place in Southeast Finland, where large-scale agriculture was undertaken in the donated lands. It appears that here (as also in Ostrobothnia) the peasant community was less accustomed to the measures and practices of the nobility than their colleagues in the coastal zone between Sibbo and Björneborg who had internalized their subjugated position. The former were easily provoked to defend their rights.[145] A further element to this Southeast Finnish manorial culture was introduced by Baltic nobles who were accustomed at home to despise the peasants and their aims. But Finnish and Swedish noblemen could act in the same manner. There were both members of the high nobility and parvenus. This was largely a question of personal choice – whether to follow the course of Christian charity and the code of the just master[146] and to seek moderation and reconciliation in order to avoid damaging and embarrassing disputes, or to let outright self-interest take precedence. The ideal and the calculations of interest easily came into conflict with each other. On the basis of the above facts it can be deduced that explanations of history solely with reference to either rationally conceived and followed interests or to ideological, mental and other structures will lead to imperfect results; both aspects must be taken into account.

---

[145] The nobles may also have regarded the level of crown taxation to be too low particularly in Southeastern Finland and in the inland regions, and therefore they began to improve their own income by the means of contractual rent, but this has not been investigated sufficiently.

[146] These are discussed in Englund's book *Det hotade huset*.

A stress on the rebelliousness of the peasants, or alternatively their subjugation, prevents one from seeing the totality of subtle practices with which the peasants pursued their interests. On his own before the nobleman or in the machinery of the crown (e.g. in court), the peasant was powerless, but in larger numbers also his views carried weight. The nobles had a great deal of power on their estates, but it was anything but limitless. Day labour became the symbol of noble authority, and the peasants who had lost their hereditary rights were powerless in this respect. On the other hand, the nobles could not do very much about the inability – or unwillingness – of the peasants to pay rent. In times of a shortage of labour it was impossible to evict all those who had accumulated arrears. The nobles largely had to accept the rent that could be obtained from the peasants.

The donated-land peasants particularly suffered from situations where their weekly labour days had been raised to two or more without any or at least any appreciable reduction of the rent laid down in the crown cadastre. This situation particularly concerned former crown peasants who had become the subjects of the nobles, while the donated-land peasants who had retained their hereditary rights managed at least after the middle of the century with the smaller amount of day labour laid down by the *Riksdag*. It appears that also the burden on the old donated-land peasants was smaller than that of the former crown peasants, because the rent paid by the former was lower than that decreed by the crown for other peasant groups. On the other hand, there is not precise knowledge of their obligations that were left unitemized. The payment burden that remained small, at least apparently but no doubt also in reality, also had a certain ideological content and function. According to it, the old donated-land peasants were under the special protection of the master. Day labour was a greater burden on the smaller donated estates such as Bjärnå, Kumogård and Meltola, where a variety of items were produced for export to Sweden, than in the large counties and baronies where day labour was easily available for the all the needs of the masters.

It is naturally impossible to objectively relate to the increased day-labour requirements the (peace-time) halved conscription requirements of the donated-land peasants in comparison with those who remained bound to the crown. But it appears that their heavy extra day-labour burden negated any benefits that they may have gained with regard to conscription. This, however, did not apply to the donated-land peasants who had preserved their hereditary rights, who had the latter benefits in addition to a small amount of day labour. The tax peasants of the donated lands had a smaller total burden than any other peasant groups: both the donated-land peasants who had lost their hereditary rights and the tax and crown peasants remaining bound to the crown. Despite this, the estate of the peasants spoke vociferously at the *Riksdag* of the claimed particularly endangered and poor position of the tax peasants on donated lands!

It was largely the personal choice of the noble landlord whether he chose to seize all benefits that could be had from his peasants or whether he wanted to avoid problems and keep to the role of the fair landlord. The former model of behaviour was common on the properties of the Baltic nobility and in the inland regions of Finland, where low crown taxes were incentive to raise rents. The peasants of the periphery were presumably more prepared to defend their interests than the inhabitants of the coastal regions. Where relations between the manor and its peasants had become enflamed, the conflicts tended to go on indefinitely and would flare up from time to time. The policy of appropriation led to passive resistance among the peasants, and was probably no more profitable for the master than compromise would have been.

It should be noted that taxation did not have a purely negative effect on the personal economy of the peasants (i.e. the transfer of the resources produced by them to the crown or to a nobleman). Taxation forced the peasant to improve the management and production of his holding. This was most clearly obvious in the peasant-based production of tar in Ostrobothnia, with which funds were obtained for the payment of taxes and the hiring of substitute soldiers to serve the crown.[147] In Southwest Finland it is not so easy to see the positive effects of 17th-century taxation, even though there must have been such effects at least in marginal terms. An obstacle was posed by the incompatibility of day-labour services and the structure of peasant-based agricultural production. Day labour for the nobles, in lieu of taxes or rent, impaired the peasants' management of their own households and particularly their additional means of livelihood, thus impeding adaptation to taxation (i.e. rents).

---

[147]   Villstrand, *Anpassning eller protest*, pp. 219–244.

ABANDONED FARMS AND THE SURVIVAL STRATEGIES OF THE PEASANTS (AN EXCURSION INTO THE DIVERSITY OF RELATIONS BETWEEN THE CROWN, NOBILITY AND PEASANTS)

ABANDONED FARMS

Inability to pay tax officially ratified by the crown entailed three kinds of easements (instalments). 1) An abandoned holding or farm (*ödehemman*) was a holding whose resident had died or moved away, or had simply been declared unable to pay taxes despite being alive and living on the property. 2) Holdings taken under cultivation (*upptagna*) on the basis of tax-exempt years, i.e. temporary tax exemption, consisted of both former abandoned farms and new holdings for which no tax had ever been paid. The latter were rare in Southwest Finland. 3) Reduced-rate (*förmedlade*) holdings had been awarded a reduction of tax for their *mantal* units, thus paying tax according to a lower *mantal* figure than before the reduction. The latter group included appended (*inlagda*) holdings or parts of such, the taxes of which was foregone by the crown to be paid to another farm in order to aid and strengthen it.[148]

---

[148]   On the lists of instalments and the concept of the abandoned farm, see e.g. Ilkka Mäntylä, 'Kronan och undersåtarnas svält,' *Karolinska förbundets årsbok* 1988, pp. 48–50

The lists of instalments and abandoned holdings of the Province of Åbo and Björneborg, which are in satisfactory condition from 1663 onwards[149], reveal the fact, strange at first sight, that the coastal parishes of Nykyrko, Letala, Lappi and Ulvsby had a particularly large number of abandoned farms that had been officially noted as being unable to pay tax. In 1663, their proportion of all *mantal* units was 33.5% in Nykyrko, 30.5% in Letala, 36.0% in Lappi and 23.4% in Ulvila. Of the other parishes in the province only S:t Mårtens exceeded 30% in this respect (34.6%). Many of these abandoned farms in the coastal regions were literally abandoned, i.e. without inhabitants and had possibly been so for a long while. The lists of arrears of 1663 and subsequent years show that some of the inhabitants of the coastal areas had gone to sea, to Stockholm or other parts of Sweden to gain their livelihood or to earn money to pay their arrears to the nobles by working in other, non-agricultural, capacities outside their farms.[150]

The wars, crop failures and raised taxes of the early 17th century were without doubt the main individual reason for the abandonment of farm, but the fact that holdings in the coastal region remain abandoned also reflects the condition that, unlike the inland, this region offered sources of income outside the agricultural sector. In other words, the high percentages of

---

or the same author's *Kruunu ja alamaisten nälkä: 1690-luvun katovuosien verotulojen vähennys Pohjanmaalla ja esivallan vastatoimenpiteet* (Oulu, 1988), pp. 9–24. Also Antti Kujala, 'Talonpoikien veronmaksukyvyn kehitys Turun ja Porin sekä Uudenmaan ja Hämeen lääneissä 1694–1712,' *Historiallinen Aikakauskirja* 1999, pp. 5–13. Studies on abandoned farms related to previous centuries: Eljas Orrman, *Bebyggelsen i Pargas, S:t Mårtens och Vemo socknar i Egentliga Finland under senmedeltiden och på 1500-talet* (Helsingfors, 1986); Anneli Mäkelä, *Hattulan kihlakunnan ja Porvoon läänin autioitumi-nen myöhäiskeskiajalla ja uuden ajan alussa* (Helsinki, 1979).

149 The lists of instalments for certain administrative districts in the Province of Åbo and Björneborg include at times in the 1660s the class of indigent (*oförmögna*) alongside the categories of abandoned, taken under cultivation and reduced. In Tables 3–4 their *mantal* units are added to those of the abandoned farms. For example, the lists of instalments for 1660 do not include abandoned, recultivated and reduced farms/*mantals* under the authority of the nobles. KA, 7279.

150 KA, 7288, 7289 & 7292 (cadastre 1663, verification books 1663 & 1664).

abandoned properties of the late 17th century did not reflect any exceptional economic distress but an abundance of economic alternatives alongside difficulties.

With regard to abandonment and other forms of inability to pay tax the first half of the 17th century is not discussed here, but information from the Barony of Kimito and Per Brahe's Juva manor at S:t Mårtens clearly shows that the number of abandoned farms and *mantals* was considerably larger in the first half and middle of the century than in the latter half.[151] In 1631 in Lower Satakunta the proportion of abandoned farms of all holdings was 41%, but in 1649 this figures was "only" 27%. The largest proportions in 1631 and 1649 were at Ulvsby (53/41% respectively) and Kumo (50/46%). According to Mikko Huhtamies, these settled parishes had the relatively highest tax burden of Lower Satakunta and in comparison with the periphery of the region only a small amount of land suitable for clearing. In addition, the area had an agricultural economy focusing on unproductive grain farming instead of animal husbandry and a poorly functioning and unfair system of conscription caused by local social structure. Together, these factors all promoted the process of abandonment.[152]

Of the *mantal* units of Ulvsby Parish belonging to the County of Björneborg 32.5% were abandoned in 1668, while 48.0% had been granted tax exemption on the grounds of abandonment or because of being taken under cultivation. The respective figures for all the *mantal* units in the whole parish were only 17.1% and 24.0% in the same year.[153] The abandoned farms, however, were

151   Gardberg, *Kimito friherreskap*, p. 99. On the estate of Juva in S:t Mårtens see above. On the counties and baronies and their decreasing degree of abandonment 1650–1675, see Jokipii, *Suomen kreivi- ja vapaaherrakunnat*, I, s. 210–213 (199–219, 391).

152   Mikko Huhtamies, *Sijaissotilasjärjestelmä ja väenotot: Taloudellis-sosiaalinen tutkimus sijaissotilaiden käytöstä Ala-Satakunnan väenotoissa vuosina 1631–1648* (Helsinki, 2000), p. 126 (124–148); Mauno Jokipii, *Satakunnan historia*, IV (s.l., 1974), pp. 680–686 and passim.

153   RA, Bielkesamlingen, Jordebok 1668, E 2425 (vol. 29, KA, FR 200); KA, 7305 & 7307 (1668). Only a bare 1 ½ *mantal* units in the whole parish were under the provisions of reduction (*förmedling*), the third instalment based on inability to pay tax.

not solely or primarily a problem of donated lands. In other areas, such as for example the administrative district (*härad*) of Pikis they were proportionately more numerous on land paying their taxes to the crown. In 1663 the abandoned holdings of the district of Pikis concentrated in the coastal parishes of Pargas and Nagu.[154] On the other hand, Kimito Parish (in the Barony of Kimito), which was also in the archipelago, had a relatively small number of abandoned *mantal* units.[155]

Table 3. Percentage of abandoned *mantal* units of all *mantal* units in the administrative districts of Vemo and Pikis and the upper district of Upper Satakunta and the parishes of Nykyrko, Letala, Lappi, S:t Mårtens and Ulvsby

	Vemo district	Nykyrko Letala	Lappi	Pikis district	S:t Mårtens	Ulvsby	upper district, Upper Satakunta
1663	23,4	32,5	36,0	8,7	34,6	23,4	9,5
1666	19,2	26,1	33,2	7,9	24,0	21,1	7,2
1668	19,2	27,0	32,5	7,6	23,2	17,1	4,4
1670	18,8	26,0	31,3	8,2	25,4	18,4	4,4
1672	20,0	27,6	32,2	8,2	25,9	17,3	4,4
1674	24,3	35,6	37,3	7,2	25,2	12,3	3,7
1676	26,2	38,1	38,8	8,2	25,8	14,6	4,7
1678	31,0	47,5	35,5	9,9	31,3	16,5	4,6
1680	25,1	39,9	26,9	9,1	20,0	14,7	5,5
1682	18,4	27,5	22,9	8,7	18,4	16,5	5,9
1684	16,2	24,3	20,3	6,7	13,0	13,4	5,8
1686	16,8	24,4	23,8	5,1	9,8	12,8	6,0
1689	11,0	18,1	10,1	3,9	8,4	8,7	4,5

Source: Cadastres and verification books of the provincial accounts (lists of instalments)[156]

---

[154]   KA, 7289, p. 153 ff.
[155]   Gardberg, *Kimito friherreskap*, p. 99.
[156]   Letala-Nyrkyrko 1664: KA, 7314 (1670), p. 259.

Table 4. Percentage of *mantal* units abandoned, taken under cultivation and reduced /abandoned *mantal* units of all *mantal* units in the administrative districts of the Province of Åbo and Björneborg with the exception of the Åland Islands

	Vemo district	Nykyrko Letala parishes	Masku district	Pikis district	Halikko district	Lower Satakunta	upper district, Upper Satakunta	lower district, Upper Satakunta
1670	24,7/18,8	29,3/26,0	17,5/6,5	13,4/8,2	14,6/9,2	15,7/10,5	7,4/4,4	13,5/9,1
1680	32,5/25,1	48,7/39,9	24,7/8,6	22,0/9,1	22,9/8,6	17,9/10,9	11,4/5,5	21,1/9,1
1689	25,9/11,0	30,7/18,1	22,7/5,0	18,6/3,9	20,2/3,9	12,3/4,7	13,8/4,5	16,9/6,9

Source: As in the previous table. Figures for 1669 instead of 1670 for the administrative district of Halikko.

Tables 3 and 4[157] show that the number of abandoned holdings and *mantal* units decreased after 1663. There were several years of crop failure around the middle of the 1670s and therefore the number of abandoned *mantals* again began to rise. In the 1680s, donated lands began to be restituted to the crown. As shown by the few abandoned *mantal* units of the parish and Barony of Kimito, some of the nobles sought to make the abandoned holdings capable of paying taxes with measures equal to the crown and with even greater success. In this area, however, the crown was more active than the nobles on the average and it had more means at its disposal. Therefore, the number of abandoned *mantal* units decreased in all parts of the country from the 1680s until the great crop failure and famine years of the 1690s.

Table 3 presents the areas of large numbers of abandoned *mantal* units, the administrative district of Vemo and its parishes of Nykyrko, Letala and Lappi, where the abandoned properties were particularly concentrated, and from other parts of the

---

[157] Owing to the confusing and unestablished procedure temporarily caused by new (as yet few) levyings of tax it is very difficult to calculate the total *mantal* figures for administrative district and parishes for the years 1684–1689. Therefore I have used on their part in Tables 3 and 4 the total *mantal* figures for 1682.

province Ulvsby and S:t Mårtens, which also distinguished themselves as parishes with a large number of abandoned farms. For the sake of comparison, the table also includes the administrative district of Pikis representing the settled coastal areas and the peripheral upper administrative district of Upper Satakunta in the inland. Before the last years of the 17th century, high abandoned *mantal* figures in the Province of Åbo and Björneborg were a problem particularly of certain coastal areas, but not of the inland, which still relied partly on slash-and-burn farming and was regarded as being undeveloped. It must therefore be investigated why there were constantly so many abandoned holdings in these areas. A partial answer to this question is the above-mentioned existence of means of livelihood alternative to farming in the coastal regions, but this alone is not enough. Further investigation requires a closer look particularly at the County of Vasaborg.

THE COUNTY OF VASABORG AS BOTH TAX HELL AND TAX HAVEN

The County of Vasaborg (most of Nykyrko and Letala Parishes and the town of Nystad) had been donated in 1646 to Gustav Gustavsson, King Gustavus II Adolphus's (1611–1632) son born out of wedlock. After the death of Gustav Gustavsson in 1653, the county passed on to his widow Anna Sofia.[158]

The county contained 704 holdings and 586 ¼ *mantal* units of the total of 680 ¼ *mantal* units in the parishes of Nykyrko and Letala in the administrative district of Vemo. According to the

---

[158]   RA, Kammararkivet, Reduktionskollegii akter, F I:127, Gustav Gustavsson (KA, FR 1054); RA, Kammararkivet, Grev- och friherreskap, Vasaborg; Kyösti Kaukovalta, *Uudenkaupungin historia*, I (Tampere, 1917), pp. 101–109; Robert Swedlund, *Grev- och friherreskapen i Sverige och Finland: Donationerna och reduktionerna före 1680* (Uppsala, 1936), pp. 70, 273. Also Jokipii's *Suomen kreivi- ja vapaaherrakunnat* I–II discusses the County of Vasaborg.

Saari manor in Virmo, present-day Mietoinen, belonged to Gustav Gustavsson as from the end of 1630s. The manor was later administered in conjunction with the County of Vasaborg which Gustav Gustavsson obtained in 1646. During restitution, Saari returned to the crown. Augustin Ehrensvärd, constructor of Sveaborg, died in his Saari residence in 1772. The manor house was destroyed in a fire in 1773, and the new building in the photo was built towards the end of the same decade. Photo: A. Kujala.

general ledger of the crown for 1655, the holdings appended to Vasaborg provided a total of 13,308 silver dalers in annual and uncertain taxes etc. In addition there were also the county's shares of extraordinary taxes, income from Nystad and separately the annual and uncertain taxes to the amount of 3,376 dalers from Saari manor in the parish of Virmo.[159] Owing to the considerable number of abandoned properties in Nykyrko and Letala and

---

[159]   KA, 7257, pp. 31–32, 91.

because of arrears, the actual rent yield was considerably smaller. In 1658 and again in 1663 and 1667, Anna Sofia, who was in possession of the county, was completely exempted from the quarter tax, which meant a tax-exemption income of 3,182 dalers on the part of Vasaborg and 843 dalers for Saari manor in Virmo.[160] In 1673 the County of Vasaborg had to relinquish a quarter of its appended holdings in the one-quarter restitution that was enacted for it.[161]

In 1680, around the time when the restitution of the county took place 39.9% (vs. 32.5% in 1663) of *mantal* units were abandoned in Nykyrko and Letala, and as many as 48.7% of all *mantal* units could not provide tax or rent because of exemption granted for abandoned status or other economic distress. In fact, things were developing in a more positive direction at the time, as two years earlier, in 1678, the proportion of abandoned *mantal* units of all *mantal* units was as much as 47.5% and that of abandoned, those taken under cultivation and reduced (non-tax paying) *mantal* units was 51.3% of the total.[162] The peak figures of 1678 were the result of severe crop failure in the mid-1670s (particularly in 1674–1676)[163] and the disturbances caused by war with Denmark in 1675–1679 (labour shortages caused by conscription and problems of trade) as well as the fact that the crown tightened its grip on the County of Vasaborg. The crown now carried out the one-quarter restitution of holdings in 1673.

---

[160] KA, 7295, pp. 1066–1071; RA, Kammararkivet, Reduktionskollegii akter, F I:127, Gustav Gustavsson (KA, FR 1054).
[161] KA, 7323, p. 106.
[162] KA, 7342, 7344 a-b, 7348 & 7350 (cadastre and verification books 1678, 1680).
[163] RA, Rydboholmssamlingen, Wrangelska godshandlingar, Bjärnå, Ordinarie härads vinterting 13.–14.2.1674 & 27.–28.1.1679, vols 476 & 548, E 7942 & 8014 (the first-mentioned excerpt as an appendix to a letter from P. Hackes); RA, Bielkesamlingen, Gustav Horn och Sigrid Bielke, Ordinarie härads höstting, Vittis, 30.9.–2.10.1674 & P. Påhlsson to S. Bielke 25.1., 3.3., 6.4. & 28.8.1675 & 30.8.1676, E 2385, P. Påhlsson to J. Gernman 16.8.1674 & 4.3.1675, E 2386 (KA, FR 197–198); RA, Landshövdingars skrivelser till K.M:t, Åbo och Björneborgs län, vols 1–2, H. Oxe 12.9.1674, 30.5.1677 & 13.5.1678 (KA, FR 41–42).

The taxes from these holdings were now assigned to the armed forces. As part of these changes a large number of new holdings were recorded as abandoned in comparison with the situation in 1677. The crown apparently noted that these properties were so badly managed and unable to pay taxes that improvements had to be launched with an outright purge. In the parish of Lappi, also belonging to the administrative district of Vemo, the number of abandoned *mantal* units peaked in 1677 (39.4%), no doubt partly because of the same reasons related to military service.[164] Since the proportion of abandoned *mantal* units also reached a very high figure at S:t Mårtens in 1678, there is reason to assume that war and crop failure were the main reasons for the peak of abandoned-holding figures in the province. Alongside crop failure there were other causes in the administrative district of Vemo, which are discussed in more detail below.

In all other parts of the province the proportion of abandoned *mantal* units was still lower in 1680 than in 1663. One reason for reversed trend in Nykyrko and Letala and the large numbers of abandoned *mantal* units in general in the above coastal parishes was the lack of tax reductions (*förmedlingar*). Before the 1670s, they had not been granted practically speaking at all in the County of Vasaborg (any more than in Lappi or the part of Ulvsby Parish belonging to the County of Björneborg). It was the policy of the crown to grant tax reduction or remission for arrears on donated land only if the nobleman concerned first granted a corresponding reduction, which meant that the peasants of Vasaborg did not receive remissions for the unduly high taxes any more from their masters than from the crown.

During its last years in the late 1670s, the County of Vasaborg was the scene of restlessness, no doubt caused at least partly by the economic problems of the time. In 1678 a lay member of the district court in Letala was reluctant to collect arrears due to the

[164] KA, verification books for the years concerned.

county from the peasants. He stated that he does not care for the affairs of the count (countess) and expressed his contempt for the countess by snapping his fingers. The court sessions punished him with a fine of 40 marks.[165] In 1679, some of the peasants of Vasaborg who had passed on to the crown in the one-quarter restitution of 1673 did not want to participate in the investigation of their arrears from the time of the county. They apparently felt that these arrears no longer concerned them. In an official proclamation read in the churches of the region they were ordered to appear at the investigation in order to avoid legal penalties.[166]

Nykyrko, Letala and Lappi belonged to the administrative district of Vemo, and in the 1660s–1680s a larger proportion of the *mantal* units of this district were classed as abandoned than in any other administrative district in the Province of Åbo and Björneborg. However, in calculating the average burden of all crown taxes (including extraordinary taxes) per *mantal* unit for 1670 and assuming that the nobles levied all that the crown had chosen not to,[167] the tax and rent burden per *mantal* unit in the administrative district of Vemo (33.7 silver dalers) was lower than in any other administrative distict of the province. The natural explanation for this paradox is that the *mantal* rate in the district was "lower" than the average rate for the province, i.e. it was based on lower economic potential and ability to pay taxes than elsewhere.[168]

---

165 Jokipii, *Suomen kreivi- ja vapaaherrakunnat*, II, p. 201.
166 KA, judicial district of Vemo and Lower Satakunta I, judgment book 1679, p. 25 (Letala summer district court sessions 14.–15.7.1679).
167 KA, 7312–7314 a. As was already seen, this assumption is not completely correct, but there is no other possibility.
168 This was due not only to unduly high taxes per se but also to the fact that many of the inhabitants of the administrative district of Vemo had undertaken other means of livelihood instead of farming.

Table 5. The tax burden per *mantal* unit including instalments in the administrative districts of the Province of Åbo and Björneborg in silver dalers in 1670

	Annual	Uncert.	Extraord.	Total
Vemo	12.1	11.2	10.4	33.7
Masku	12.6	12.5	10.5	35.7
Pikis	14.5	13.0	10.3	37.7
Halikko	13.4	12.4	10.0	35.8
Lower SK	14.1	15.1	10.5	39.7
Upper SK upper	9.9	14.9	11.0	35.8
Upper SK lower	11.4	14.9	10.9	37.2

Source: KA, 7312–7314 a (cadastre, general ledger and verification books for 1670).[169]

In 1688 the crown instituted new tax levies to lower the taxes of holdings restituted to it, and the largest tax reductions in the Province of Åbo and Björneborg were carried out at the time in

---

[169] An annual rent was calculated for the old donated land in accordance with its *mantal* figures because it did not have any annual rent in the crown cadastres. The proportion of the old donated land was doubled for the uncertain taxes, because the crown recorded only half of the uncertain taxes (this was purely a relic of book-keeping, because the nobles collected in any case all the uncertain taxes of their estates). The proportion of livestock fees and transport fees for donated land was also multiplied by two, because the nobles collected the other half of them for themselves. Tithes and judge taxes are included among the uncertain taxes (where they did not belong). This group also includes a small group of revenue that was not taxes (fines among others). In the crown accounts, they were included among the regular taxes. They were not removed owing to their small amount. In keeping with crown practice, poll tax was included in the extraordinary taxes. The figures show that higher uncertain taxes, including tithes etc., were decreed for Satakunta than for Finland-Proper. As a peripheral inland area, the upper administrative district of Upper Satakunta was assigned a relatively low annual rent. The calculation does not take into account tax exemption granted for abandoned conditions or other inability to pay tax, because this would make the whole calculation almost impossible. Moreover, when calculating the overall burden it is necessary also to calculate taxes that proved to be insurmountable to their payers. In 1660 the tax burden per *mantal* unit in Northern Ostrobothnia was clearly lower than in the Province of Åbo and Björneborg in 1670. Virrankoski, 'Pohjois-Pohjanmaa ja Lappi 1600-luvulla', pp. 465–473.

the administrative district of Vemo, where the need for them appears to have been greatest.[170]

The archives of the County of Vasaborg have disappeared, which makes it difficult to draw conclusions. It is, however, obvious that it sufficed for the countess to have rent and other income from the county. The granting of tax reductions, the abandoned status of holdings as the result of unduly high taxes (rents) and the creation of new tax-payers through temporary tax exemptions did not interest the countess, who lived outside Finland. This led to almost record-high numbers of abandoned *mantal* units and the growth of abandoned *mantals*, while in other parts of the province developments took an opposite course in the late 1660s and at the end of the following decade.

So much for the tax hell of the peasants. The County of Vasaborg was, however, also a tax haven, or paradise, for its residents,

---

[170] KA, 7387–7388 (1691).The reduction in tax can be seen not only in ready money but also in the decrease in the number of the farms and *mantals* as tax-paying units (regular cadastre minus extraordinary instalments plus miscellaneous cadastre). In the administrative district of Vemo in 1691 taxes decreased 19.5% in comparison with taxes collected before the new levyings. Changes in the regional division of the administrative districts in 1690 make comparisons difficult. However, the comparisons can be made along the borders of the new division but still with the figures before the regular cadastre that was in force before the new levyings.The largest tax reductions in the administrative district of Vemo were specifically carried out in the parishes of Letala and Nykyrko. (In 1690 the parish of Lappi was removed from the district of Vemo to Lower Satakunta). Reductions of this magnitude were not achieved in any other administrative district. In Upper Satakunta and in the new administrative district of Virmo taxes increased as new farms came under taxation. In the administrative district of Virmo this change was largely due to the fact that in the district of Masku, in the area of which it was established, half of the old donated land, i.e. ca. 120 *mantal* units, were noted during the 1680s to be other than old donated land, and an annual rent was also laid down for these properties in the crown accounts (and their uncertain taxes doubled).This raising of taxes was a raise for the crown but not for the peasants. A similar trend in reductions of tax continued after 1691. See also Kujala, 'Talonpoikien veronmaksukyvyn kehitys Turun ja Porin sekä Uudenmaan ja Hämeen lääneissä 1694–1712,' pp. 22–23 and 'Why Did Finland's War Economy Collapse during the Great Northern War?,' pp. 79–82. An example of the many reasons for tax reductions is given in Orrman, 'Säteribildningen i Finland under 1600-talet,' p. 290. In 1690 the province divided into nine administrative districts instead of the former eight to facilitate tax collection. RA, Kammarkollegium till K.M:t, vol. 38, 9.11.1689.

where taxes were evaded as much as possible. These skills were also known elsewhere in the province and throughout the realm.

In 1668—1670 Johan Ekholm, an official of the Chamber College inspected tax evasion among the inhabitants of the Province of Åbo and Björneborg. This was practised through the unauthorized and unrecompensed farming of abandoned farms, and by concealing livestock and not officially recording hired hands. Occasionally, the nobles were paid compensation for illicit farming. In the parish of Nyrkyrko in 1667—1668 there was clandestine cultivation in 30 *mantal* units, i.e. one out of every five abandoned *mantal* units. The culprits agreed to pay a "voluntary" fine in order to avoid more serious repercussions.[171]

Restitution was carried out on the part of the County of Vasaborg in 1681, and together with a number of baronies in the archipelago it was subject to the Swedish admiralty, i.e. its farms had to pay their taxes to the navy. Niklas Mallenius, inspector of the admiralty, immediately saw why, and on what conditions so many of the holdings in the county were abandoned. Old farmers without means lived on the abandoned farms, or they were literally abandoned, or even grown over with forest or appended to the lands of their neighbours. This was quite normal. In addition, there were, however, farmers who had gone to sea and – even stranger – those who could have worked on the farms with regard to their age and health. But they did not even have domestic animals and they earned their livelihood in keeping with local tradition by making wooden vessels and containers and selling them to burghers. Their farms could remain in an abandoned state or they could obtain temporary tax exemption without, however, improving the farm to be cultivated, which was the purpose of tax exemption.

In other words, they evaded taxes in all possible ways, and in complete agreement with the county. The crafts practised on a cottage-industry basis had namely also benefited the economy of

---

[171]   KA, 7311 (1669), pp. 1653–1763.

the county through the small duty levied on products taken to town of Nystad to be sold. From 1646 until 1656 and from 1665 to 1678 Nystad belonged to the county, and the nobleman in possession of the county received half of all the small duty.

Mallenius made the admiralty levy higher tax-rate prices (*markegångspris*) on the peasants' tax items than the so-called crown values in use in the crown´s system of taxation. During the period of Vasaborg County the peasants had become used to paying their rent in ready cash, thus obtaining a discount on their rent. Now the tax-rate prices of the admiralty raised their taxes. In early 1682 the peasants began to disobey. Hardly any taxes could be obtained from them and they did not obey Mallenius's order to come and pay their taxes on specially arranged occasions. The inspector complained to the admiralty that nothing could be obtained from the peasants except by force, but even this was not possible, because Provincial Governor Oxe, who was strict about his own domain of power would not let the inspector resort to the authority to confiscate property and other measures reserved for crown officials.

The peasants, of course, did not like to pay the relatively high small duty on their wooden vessels, but the government did not pay heed to their complaints about this at the *Riksdag*. It is even probable that restrictions on peasant seafaring for the benefit of the ports of Nystad and Raumo led to the abandonment of holdings in the administrative district of Vemo.

A great deal of wooden vessels were also made in the parish of Lappi. The manufacture of them and other wooden products for sale and the joint sources of income provided by the seaman's occupation and both legal and illegal peasant seafaring explain why Lappi followed the course of Nykyrko and Letala in high abandonment figures. In the district of Vemo seafaring for the purpose of trade with Sweden was permitted for the inhabitants of Pyhämaa, the archipelago of the administrative parishes of Nykyrko and Letala (and also for the inhabitants of Tövsala Parish). The inhabitants of the archipelago could in a completely legal manner take their vessels and containers for sale to Sweden without having to sell them to the burghers of Nystad or Raumo. The wooden vessels were made of aspen and alder and this source of income was available only to those peasants who had forests where aspen and alder grew.[172] Of the towns of Finland, only Åbo, Helsingfors and Viborg had staple rights, i.e. were entitled to engage in foreign trade. The government concentrated the trade and seafaring of the towns of the Gulf of Bothnia in Stockholm. Åbo was designated to be the other port to be used, although it could not compete in any way with the capital of the realm. The burghers of Björneborg, Raumo and Nystad were, however, allowed to export lumber and wooden vessels to Germany, but only money and salt could be brought back on the return journey. The burghers of Nystad also sailed to Denmark and South Sweden.[173]

The peak in abandonment figures in 1677—1678 at Nyrkyrko, Letala and Lappi was apparently largely due to crop failure, resulting epidemics and war with Denmark. Not only contributing to a shortage of labour everywhere because of conscription, the war also greatly hindered seafaring in the southern parts of the

---

[172] Krigsarkivet, Stockholm, Amiralitetskollegiet, kansliet, Inkomna handlingar, 1681, vol. 2, pp. 392–395, 1682, vol. 1, pp. 545, 558–560, N. Mallenius to the College of the Admiralty 9.7.1681 & 23.3.1682. See also Gardberg, *Kimito friherreskap*, pp. 282–293; RA, Landshövdingars skrivelser till K.M:t, Åbo och Björneborgs län, vol. 3, L. Creutz 2.8.1684 (KA, FR 42). On the making and sale of wooden vessels and related tariffs, see Kauko-valta, *Uudenkaupungin historia*, I, pp. 112, 143–147, 159–170; Yrjö Hormia, *Pyhämaan-Pyhärannan 300-vuotisvaiheita* (Rauma, 1939), pp. 46, 105–107; P. Papunen, *Rauman seudun historia*, I (Rauma, 1959), pp. 370–396; Olavi Koivisto, *Laitilan historia*, I (Vamma-la, 1969), p. 366; Jokipii, *Suomen kreivi- ja vapaaherrakunnat*, II, pp. 7–9; RA, Kammararkivet, Reduktionskollegii akter, F I:127, Gustav Gustavsson (KA, FR 1054) (containing an investigation of the estates of Vasaborg and Saari on 24.10.1671, noting the nature of the property of the peasants, including their forests). Eero Kling has observed that the peasants of Vasaborg addressed their complaints to the *Riksdag* instead of their landlords, correctly noting this to be an indication of Anna Sofia's lack of interest in the county, which was common knowledge. Eero Kling, *"Stormechtigste Konungh, Allernådigste Herre": Rahvaan valitukset 1600–1680, lähitarkastelussa Vehmaan kihlakunta ja Vaasaporin krei-vikunta*, unpublished MA thesis in Finnish history, University of Helsinki, 2000.

[173] Ilkka Mäntylä, 'Suurvaltakausi,' *Suomen historian pikkujättiläinen* (Porvoo, 1987), p. 250; Jokipii, *Satakunnan historia*, IV, pp. 605–609.

Pyhämaa votive church was built in the early 17th century, or even prior to that. Its structures bear resemblance to old-school medieval churches, which shows that forms of the Catholic rite had survived past the Protestant reform. Pyhämaa was part of the archipelago of the administrative parishes of Nykyrko and Letala where seafaring was a legal means of livelihood for the peasants. The seafarers donated offerings to the church to thank God for their successful voyages. Photo: A. Kujala.

Baltic, and the trade in wooden vessels from Nystad and Raumo in these areas.[174] This area of Finland was just as dependent on foreign trade as Ostrobothnia and Savolax, with their tar-burning economy.[175]

---

[174]   RA, Landshövdingars skrivelser till K.M:t, Åbo och Björneborgs län, vol. 2, H. Oxe 30.5. & 2.6.1677 & 13.5.1678 (KA, FR 42); Kaukovalta, *Uudenkaupungin historia*, I, pp. 147, 193, 209. The peak figures of abandoned farms for S:t Mårtens were apparently due to the damage and disease caused by troops passing through the parish. Orrman, *Bebyggelsen i Pargas, S:t Mårtens och Vemo socknar i Egentliga Finland under senmedeltiden och på 1500-talet*, pp. 118, 194.

[175]   Kujala, *Miekka ei laske leikkiä*, pp. 63, 67–69.

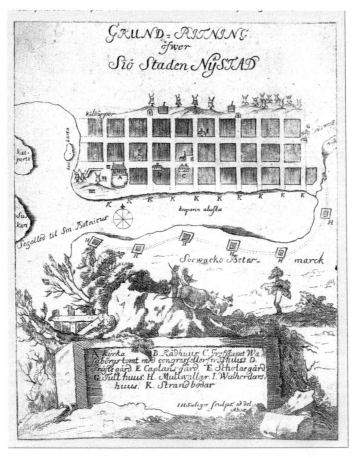

King Gustavus II Adolphus had an illegitimate son Gustav Gustavsson (1616–1653). He served as a colonel of the cavalry in the Thirty Years' War. In 1646, Queen Christina made her half-brother the Count of Vasaborg, assigning him the County of Vasaborg in Southwest Finland. The Swedish monarch endowed her "improper and ignoble" relative with generous donations but mistrusted him, keeping him well away from the chambers of power. Gustav Gustavsson spent most of his time in Germany. When visiting Nystad in 1649, the count gave orders that the town inhabitants had to unmake their houses and rebuild them on the lots shown in the town plan in this picture. Gracefully enough, he gave them one week to complete the transfer which leads us to the conclusion that it was a blessing for Sweden that this offspring of Gustavus II Adolphus never rose to the throne. The new, regular town plan was, indeed, realised but it took two years instead of one week. Krigsarkivet, Stockholm.

131

After 1678, the number of abandoned *mantal* units in the administrative district of Vemo began to decrease, and this trend continued after 1684 when Nyrkyrko and Letala were restored directly to the crown from the admiralty. It was in the interest of the crown to bring the abandoned farms again under cultivation and to have them pay taxes. The abnormal situation that existed in the County of Vasaborg had been caused by the poor administration of the county. A large number of farms had become abandoned, as no reduction had been made for their unduly high rent. It was in the interest of the peasants to let their holdings gain official abandoned status and to practice profitable cottage industries within the bounds of tax exemption thus achieved. The county at least tolerated tax evasion by the peasants, which primarily spelt disadvantages for the crown.[176]

Relations between the nobility and the peasants were generally marked by conflicts of interest, but in some cases they found common cause. The existence of substitutive livelihoods (the making of wooden vessels, taking posts as sailors on passing ships and peasant seafaring) along with the lack of control by the authorities maintained abandoned farms both here and in the parish of Lappi. Unduly high taxes were the original cause of farms becoming abandoned, and since this situation was not rectified, the substitutive livelihoods attracted the peasants like magnets. To make wooden vessels by avoiding taxes yet paying the small duty was certainly no gold mine for the peasants, but under existing conditions it was one way to keep one's head above water.

It is difficult to find any grounds for the view that the peasants were solely at the mercy of the crown and the nobles with no influence on their own affairs. Naturally not all peasants had such opportunities to evade taxes as in the County of Vasaborg,

---

[176] The crown naturally received half of the small duty of the town of Nystad, but in view of maintaining general discipline in the payment of taxes, it could not accept in principle such "tax planning", unlike the nobles. The crown often leased the collection of the small duty of Nystad to a burgher. Kaukovalta, p. 174.

which appeared to be a tax hell but was in reality a paradise in this respect. Of course, the peasants in this paradise ultimately shared the fate of Adam and Eve.

The crown was bound far too much by a way of thinking based on the inequality of the estates to support the cottage industries and crafts of the peasants in any way. After the peasants of the administrative district of Vemo had been restored to the crown, they were forced to take up farming again and to reject their wooden-vessel crafts. It is of course possible that by the end of the 17th century, as substitutive materials and production became widespread, the cottage industries were nevertheless past their prime.

THE PEASANTS AS TAX-PAYERS
TO THE CROWN DURING THE REIGN
OF CHARLES XI

THE RESTITUTION AND THE ALLOTMENT
SYSTEM

In so-called grand restitution King Charles XI of Sweden restored most of the former enfeoffments and donations of the realm to the crown. Also donated holdings on a purchased and pledged basis were restituted.

The nobles were allowed to keep the old donated properties that predated the donation system. Some of the restituted holdings remained in their possession in principle on the basis of former tax exemption, but now with the added obligation of maintaining cavalrymen for the army. Certain sections of the new donations remained unrestituted for a number of reasons. The king's favourites amassed large properties by buying land from other nobles in fear of restitution at very low prices.

The restitution was not carried out to raise the status of the peasants but to improve the economic basis of crown's finances and the armed forces.

The restituted farms were often converted into holdings related to office, or into benefices. The yield and income from the former went to those whole held the posts to which the farms or holdings were assigned and the officials, mostly military but also civilians, collected as their salary most of the taxes of the holdings assigned to their posts. The system is known as the tax-salary system or the (later) allotment system. The allotment system (Sw. *indelningsverket*) also contains, as its other element the military tenure system (*det ständiga knektehållet*). The nobility recovered its losses from the restitution to a considerable degree with salary from official positions. The peasants often paid the tax salaries in produce (grain etc.). The crown also paid its officials salaries in cash.[177]

The restitution aroused confusion and misunderstanding among the peasants. The nobles lost their right to day-labour services from the holdings that had been restituted from them to the crown. This inevitably led to the question of these services on the farms that had not yet been restituted. On the 10th of December 1683, the king informed the governor of the Province of Nyland and Tavastehus that the tax peasants of the donated lands with hereditary rights were to be exempted from excess day labour contractually demanded from them within the above-mentioned boundary limit. King Charles maintained that the peasants had originally been forced into agreements of this kind.

[177] Jutikkala, *Bonden i Finland genom tiderna*, pp. 200–207, 221–233; Anthony F. Upton, *Charles XI and Swedish Absolutism* (Cambridge, 1998), pp. 51–70; Sven Ågren, *Karl XI:s indelningsverk för armén: Bidrag till dess historia åren 1679–1697* (Uppsala, 1922); John E. Roos, *Uppkomsten av Finlands militieboställen under indelningsverkets nyorganisation 1682–1700* (Helsingfors, 1933). Also Ali Pylkkänen, *Talonpojan vainiolta sotilaan ruoka-pöytään: Tilojen ja niiden verojen osoittaminen sotilaille ja heidän perheillensä Suomessa 1636–1654* (Helsinki, 1996). The so-called tax-rate prices were primarily laid down in view of a situation in which the tax peasant wanted to pay his taxes to the holder of a salary estate in ready money instead of produce. The tax-rate prices were to be confirmed with reference to the price of the produce at places of trade in the province or administrative district. In practice, however, the tax-rate prices did not fluctuate as much as the market prices at their highest and lowest. They were a compromise between the peasants and the persons holding the offices in question, in which the strongest fluctuations of the market were dampened. On the European (German) examples of the political order created by King Charles XI, see Marc Raeff, *The Well-Ordered Police State: Social and Institutional Change through Law in the Germanies and Russia, 1600–1800* (New Haven, 1983); Stellan Dahlgren, 'Ekonomisk politik och teori under Karl XI:s regering,' *Karolinska förbundets årsbok* 1998, pp. 47–104.

Kousa was a wooden drinking vessel dating back to as early as the medieval times, manufactured for sale by the peasants in the parishes of Nykyrko, Letala and Lappi. The foreign demand for wooden tableware decreased as from the end of the 17th century as new materials gained ground. National Museum of Finland / Esa Suominen.

Donated-land tenant farmers who had lost their hereditary rights had to fulfil their former obligations particular in the old donated lands but also in other donations, but the nobles had no right to place too great a burden on them. The king ordered that recalcitrants were to be punished by making them run the gauntlet or even with the aid of soldiers.[178]

As the obligation of day-labour services for the manor ended among the restituted holdings, some of the peasants who had remained the tenant farmers of the nobles thought that this reform also applied to them. Accordingly, in 1684 the peasants of Kumogård manor refused to provide day labour, despite having been ordered to do so even through a ruling of a Court of Appeal. As noted above, the manor was first restituted to the crown and then restored to its owner.[179]

Bjärnå manor was restituted in 1686. Two years previously the provincial governor had ruled that the peasants appended to the manor who still had their hereditary rights could perform day-labour services in accordance with the ruling of the *Riksdag* after they had paid their arrears. Some of the peasants within the boundary limit at Bjärnå manor presented this ruling at the district court sessions in 1684, claiming that it applied to them. Upon the application of the manor lessee Lundh, the court ruled that the appellants were not only donated-land peasants but also crofters (*torpare*). In reality, they did not have hereditary rights, but in other respects the definition did not square with earlier documents concerning their holdings. The change was dictated by the interests of the manor. During the 17th century some of the boundary peasants descended to the level of mere crofters. The court maintained that there could no question whatsoever of restoring the hereditary rights of the peasants or of reducing their day-labour services in the manner proposed by them through paying their arrears. Lundh also made reference to the fact that in the cadastre the boundary peasants had been ordered to pay only

---

[178] KA, Karl XI:s registratur 1683 (avskrift), to A. Rosenhane 10.12.1683; Katajala, *Suomalainen kapina*, p. 344.

[179] KA, judicial district of Lower Satakunta II, judgment book 1684, p. 530 (Kumo winter district court sessions 1.–4.3.1684); Roos, *Uppkomsten av Finlands militieboställen under indelningsverkets nyorganisation 1682–1700*, p. 110.

half of the uncertain and extraordinary taxes, and that their day labour compensated for this reduction of payment.[180]

Colonel Georg Johan Maijdell, commander of the Tavastian Infantry Regiment was given the restituted *säter* estate of Gammel(by)gård in the parish of Borgå as his office-related estate. The allotment-system commission estimated the yield, i.e. rent, of the holding to be smaller than the amount recorded in the cadastre. Accordingly, the person in possession of the estate was entitled to corresponding compensation to his overall salary from other sources, which was a profitable solution. The salary sum, misleadingly termed rent, produced by the holding also contained two weekly labour days provided by each of the six peasants appended to it. Maijdell was also awarded the taxes paid by the above peasants with the exception of their day-labour fees, which were compensated with day labour. The peasants complained of their heavy day-labour burden first to the provincial governor, then to the district court and finally to the *Riksdag* via their representatives. From the *Riksdag* the matter went via the king to the Chamber College in 1689.

The College felt that the compensation awarded to the peasants for their large amount of day labour was too small. On the other hand, the estate was in poor condition and could not be restored without the day-labour services. Accordingly the College proposed that Maijdell's rent was to be reduced with a sum equivalent to the day-labour fees of the peasants. The latter was added to the peasants' taxes and they were exempted from the above-mentioned two weekly labour days. The king gave his blessing to the proposal of the College, which benefited the peasants more than Maijdell, as the former were exempted from their heavy, yet half-uncompensated day-labour services.[181]

---

[180] RA, Rydboholmssamlingen, Wrangelska godshandlingar, Bjärnå, Ordinarie härads vinterting 20.–21.1.1684, vol. 548, E 8014; Jutikkala, *Läntisen Suomen kartanolaitos Ruotsin vallan viimeisenä aikana*, I, p. 29.
[181] RA, Kammarkollegium till K.M:t, vol. 38, 18.10.1689; Roos, *Uppkomsten av Finlands militieboställen under indelningsverkets nyorganisation 1682–1700*, pp. 252, 321.

The question of day-labour services involved the workforce of the manors. Inasmuch as the restitution did away with day labour, the large estates had to hire farmhands or arrange crofters on their land. As early as 1685, the commoners of the Province of Åbo and Björneborg were forbidden to travel to the Baltic provinces or to Sweden. The additional purpose of this was naturally to obtain new farmers for the abandoned farms.[182] On November 18, 1693, a new royal order was issued forbidding farmhands, farm maids and other persons officially listed as vagrants from leaving the country without a passport.[183] Arvid Horn, acting governor of the Province of Åbo and Björneborg complained in 1681 to the king that there were crofters on the estates in Satakunta who had not been recorded in the crown cadastre, but provided day-labour services and paid contractual rent to their masters. In connection with conscription, the masters claimed that the crofts were on *säter*-estate land thus exempting them from conscription.[184] In Upper Satakunta, a number of crofters who were transferred to crown land in the restitution were made to pay taxes as farmers of newly cultivated land.

The organization of the allotment and military tenure system was the prime task of the provincial governors during the 1680s and at the beginning of the following decade. Restitution gave the crown tax revenue with which the armed forces and their economic basis could be given the most solid foundation possible.[185] The statements and official letters sent by the Chamber College to the king in matters related to Finland towards the end of the 17th century are dominated by a tendency to maintain

---

[182] RA, Landshövdingars skrivelser till K.M:t, Åbo och Björneborgs län, vol. 4, L. Creutz 23.5.1685 (KA, FR 42).

[183] A. A. von Stiernman (ed.), *Samling utaf Kongl. Bref, Stadgar och Förordningar Angående Sveriges Rikes Commerce, Politie och Oeconomie*, V (Stockholm, 1766), pp. 435–436.

[184] RA, Landshövdingars skrivelser till K.M:t, Åbo och Björneborgs län, vol. 2, A. Horn to Charles XI 20.8.1681 (KA, FR 42).

[185] See Roos, *Uppkomsten av Finlands militieboställer under indelningsverkets nyorganisation 1682–1700.*

taxes at certain level in order to base the salaries and income of officers and soldiers on them. Therefore the College was, in principle, averse to any reductions of taxes, even though it understood and accepted the fact that this was often done to permit the peasants to fulfil their obligations and to provide the crown with what could be obtained in general. The allotment system was organized locally under the direction of the provincial governors. Stockholm, and King Charles XI in particular, doubted, however, that the governors and commissions misused their authority.[186]

In 1685 the king banned tax reductions (*förmedlingar*) given by the nobles for their own donated properties, except in the case of fire or similar damage. These reductions also required the crown to offer tax reductions to the peasants in question. King Charles felt that the nobles preferred to reduce the taxes and rent of their appended peasants in order to make them provide even more day labour. The king opposed the disturbances caused by the tax reductions to the allotment and military tenure systems when part of the taxes and payments reserved for a certain salary or purpose remained unpaid or unfulfilled.[187]

In 1685 Lorentz Creutz, governor of the Province of Åbo and Björneborg, was so perturbed by the attitude of the king and the Chamber College regarding tax reductions that he requested and received from King Charles assurance that the reductions of tax that he had granted in connection with organizing the allotment system would not be collected at a later date either from himself personally or from his heirs.[188]

---

[186] RA, Kammarkollegium till K.M:t, vol. 31, 29.11.1686, vol. 32, 11.1.1687, vol. 34, 3.10.1687, vol. 47, 31.10. & 12.11.1692. On the personality of the king and autocracy, see Upton, *Charles XI and Swedish Absolutism*.

[187] KA, Province accounts, general documents 6830, p. 185, Charles XI to provincial governors 29.1.1685.

[188] RA, Landshövdingars skrivelser till K.M:t , Åbo och Björneborgs län, vol. 4 , L. Creutz s.d. (1685) (KA, FR 42); KA, Karl XI:s registratur 1685 (avskrift), to the Chamber College 16.12.1685.

Skottorp castle or manor house in Halland at the border between the former Danish provinces of Halland and Skåne. Skottorp was built after 1650 according to the plans by Nicodemus Tessin the Elder, and the castle was rebuilt according to the classical ideals in the early 19th century. This was the venue in 1680 of the marriage of King Charles XI with the Danish princess Ulrika Eleonora. The engagement had taken place already in 1675 at the brink of the war between the two countries, with the promised spouses never even having met each other. The last obstacle of the wedding, almost insurmountable, was the bridegroom's stinginess: he would not be convinced by his counsellors who insisted that the bride and her relatives should be given gifts that were worthy of the king of a great power. Being a man who disliked luxury and wasteful spending, Charles chose a remote manor house as the venue for his wedding. The most important thing was, however, that this prevented the French ambassador from participating in the ceremony. Charles was sour against his ally France who had dictated the terms of the peace treaties with the enemy nations, without sufficiently consulting the Swedes on the issue. These humiliations made Charles to draw away from France and approach its enemies Holland and England. But above all, the king wanted to see Sweden stand on its own two feet, and that was why Sweden had to renew itself. Photo: A. Kujala.

In royal orders issued on October 17, 1687, to Vice-Governor Johan Creutz of the Province of Åbo and Björneborg, and the Chamber College, the king decreed that in uncertain cases where a peasant who had been granted reductions to taxes or a pardon for his arrears but still assumed to have hereditary rights it was better to let him keep these rights, for it was easier for the crown to collect its receivables from a tax peasant than from a crown peasant. The same principle applied to tax reductions granted by the nobles who possessed donations. This implies indirectly that in most cases reductions of taxes or arrears had previously resulted in the loss of hereditary rights either to the crown or the nobles. In his letter King Charles also gave instructions as to how the crown could force even peasants in possession of hereditary rights to exchange holdings if the crown needed their original property. This was by no means a question of the sanctity of tax peasant ownership. If someone wished to redeem or purchase the hereditary rights and property of an impoverished tax peasant in arrears, he would have to pay the arrears.[189]

In 1691, Lorentz Creutz, governor of the Province of Åbo and Björneborg, informed the king that the taxation units for annual rent and *mantal* units of several crown holdings included in the allotment systems had been reduced. There had been discrepancies within villages where a tax holding of the same tax-paying capability as a crown holding could have a much higher taxation-unit and *mantal*-unit figure. The governor proposed a new general levying of taxes (i.e. reassessment) in such villages. The king rejected the proposal with reference to old rulings according to which no new assessments in general were to be carried out on the tax holdings. It would, however, be possible in the case of tax holdings allotted to the army if the peasants in question were to renounce their hereditary rights.

[189] KA, 6828, pp. 166–169 (also in the register of King Charles XI on the same day). Also 6834 b, A. Hedman to L. Creutz 22.12.1694.

In 1694 the king, following the proposal of the Chamber College, permitted a new levying (i.e. reduction) of taxes also for the tax holdings in the situations that were described by Creutz in 1691. The ruling said nothing about hereditary rights, and they were presumably lost in connection with the levying. New levyings now became easier to carry out. A new form of tax reduction (*förmedling*) was instituted in the provinces of Nyland and Tavastehus and Åbo and Björneborg, involving the (partial) repeal of taxes (*avskattning*) without all the formalities of a new levying. This procedure paved the way for the military tenure system, which was intended to be permanent and was therefore rigid. The repeal of taxes was also meant to help the peasants in the distress caused by the crop failures and famines of 1696–1697.[190] In this manner, the king, who was opposed to all tax reduction as a matter of principle, gradually came to accept the idea put to him by the governors and Chamber College that taxes should be lowered where necessary even for tax holdings. The interests of the allotment system called for a reduction of unduly high taxes to prevent the crown or its officials from not receiving any taxes at all through holdings achieving abandoned status, even in spite of the fact that the system, which was meant to be permanent now came to have gaps that would be difficult to fill.

---

[190] RA, Landshövdingars skrivelser till K.M:t , Åbo och Björneborgs län, vols 9 & 13, L. Creutz 14.2.1691 ja 13.5.1697 (KA, FR 43–44); KA, 6830, s. 239, 6833, s. 34, Charles XI to L. Creutz 14.3.1691 & 19.1.1694; RA, Kammarkollegium till K.M:t, vol. 52, 15.1.1694 (2 letters); KA, Karl XI:s registratur 1691 & 1697 (avskrift), to the allotment-system commission of the Province of Åbo 8.9.1691 and to L. Creutz 10.6.1697.The new levyings of tax were slowed by the lack of surveyors, which made it necessary to resort to temporary levyings. On levying and repeal of taxes, see Kujala, 'Talonpoikien veronmaksukyvyn kehitys Turun ja Porin sekä Uudenmaan ja Hämeen lääneissä 1694–1712,' pp. 10–13, 22–23 & 'Why Did Finland's War Economy Collapse During the Great Northern War?,' pp. 80–81.

ARREARS DUE TO THE CROWN BEFORE AND
AFTER RESTITUTION

As discussed above, the nobles had to adapt everywhere to the fact that they could not collect in full the rent laid down in the crown cadastre. Instead, they had to grant reduction and to overlook arrears and even pardon them.[191]

Table 6. The debet balance, i.e crown receivables (according to the general ledgers) of the main calculation of the accounts for the Province of Åbo and Björneborg

	silver dalers
1660	94,557
1670	152,203
1680	151,225
1685	216,795
1688	383,753
1690	510,421
1695	649,683
1700	853,322

In other words, the crown's receivables began to grow considerably after the mid-1680s. The majority of the new receivables consisted of tax in arrears due from peasants.[192] A comparison of the amount of arrears is given by the fact that the crown used funds via the provincial administration to the amount of 127,052 dalers in 1670, 149,787 dalers in 1680, and 266,445 in 1691. The balances and tax arrears of the provinces of Nyland and Tavastehus and Viborg and Ostrobothnia grew in a similar fashion.

---

[191] Jutikkala, *Bonden – adelsmannen – kronan*, p. 58.
[192] This can be clearly seen for example in the balance calculation for 1688 and 1689 in the general ledger of 1689 (KA, 7382) and in the list of arrears in the third part of the 1689 verification book (7383 b).

Table 7. Crown receivables in the provinces of Nyland and Tavastehus and Viborg and Ostrobothnia in silver dalers (according to the general ledgers)

	Nyl.-Tav.	Viborg	Ostrobothnia
1680	181775	28034[193]	99294[194]
1690	535910	244080	234892
1695	521163[195]	287507	320859

The expenditure of the respective provincial administrations in 1690 amounted to 155,585 dalers in the Province of Nyland and Tavastehus, 173,600 dalers in the Province of Viborg and 101,515 dalers in the Province of Ostrobothnia.

The increase of tax arrears was naturally due to the restitution of former donated holdings and the transfer of the main part of the taxes of their peasants from the nobility to the crown. From this it can be deduced that the tax sums recorded by the crown in its cadastres in the early 17th century were far too high in relation to the ability of farms and holdings to pay.

Arrears grew despite the fact that the crown listed them only on the part of taxes immediately due (bound) to it and not for taxes that it allotted for the salaries of soldiers and officials.[196] Of the farms and holdings that it had obtained in the restitution, the crown used the majority for the latter purpose. Where prior to restitution a smaller portion of donated-land tax had been paid to the crown and since these taxes and those bound to the crown already permitted the accumulation of arrears, the beginning of the growth of tax arrears only as late as the 1680s must have

---

[193] 1679
[194] 1681
[195] 1694
[196] The salary and cavalry-service estates paid to the crown only tithes, judge taxes, poll tax, livestock fees and contributions. Gunnar Olander, *Studier över det inre tillståndet i Sverige under senare tiden av Karl XII:s regering, med särskild hänsyn till Skaraborgs län* (Göteborg, 1946), p. 148; Kujala, *Miekka ei laske leikkiä*, p. 78. An example of tax arrears receivable from a salary estate: KA, 6835, pp. 455–456.

An 18th century Finnish sauna according to J. Acerbi's *Voyage Pittoresque au Cap du Nord*. Helsinki University Library / Matti Ruotsalainen.

resulted from a stricter policy in the annulment of so-called hopeless arrears and possibly also from sagging morale in matters of paying taxes. Under the authority of the nobles, the peasants had become accustomed to leaving a reasonable portion of their rent in arrears without any problems resulting from it. The crown now inherited the reluctant taxpayers of the nobles. The inclusion of the Åland Islands in the economic organization of the Province of Åbo and Björneborg also added to the amounts of arrears in the province.

In the Province of Ostrobothnia crown receivables in 1669 were only 42,106 silver dalers. The local counties and baronies had already been restituted in 1675, after which arrears due to the crown began to grow. In 1681, King Charles XI intended to pardon all arrears on the part of Ostrobothnia, or at least those that preceded the restitution of its counties and baronies, but the Chamber College convinced him to reject such a common and unitemized revoking of all arrears. The king wanted to please the common people of Ostrobothnia by agreeing to their petition, but after the College intervened normal procedure was resumed, i.e. only such arrears that could be regarded as impossible for those concerned to pay, were annulled.[197]

Of the crown receivables of 1690 and 1694 in the Province of Nyland and Tavastehus, some 140,000 dalers were from as early as the 1650s and 1660s. Some of the general ledgers of the province accounts of the early 1690s have disappeared, but it appears that in 1692, crown receivables peaked at 564,191 dalers, after which arrears were annulled, no doubt in connection with arranging the military tenure system. The revoking of arrears here was presumably based also on the king's express wish to ease the position of the common people, which had been spurred by the crop failure experienced in Tavastia in 1690. The Chamber College had again prevented the unitemized easement of the peasants´ burden of payments, but even this body could resist easements based on investigated facts. The king's exceptional compliance with easing the position of the common people was above all an expression of royal trust towards Provincial Governor C. Bonde.[198]

---

[197] RA, Kammarkollegium till K.M:t, vol. 22, 7.5.1681, vol. 23, 18.1.1682.
[198] RA, Landshövdingars skrivelser till K.M:t, Nylands och Tavastehus län, vol. 4, C. Bonde 31.7.1690 (KA, FR 17); KA, Karl XI:s registratur 1690 (avskrift), to the Chamber College 20.8.1690; RA, Kammarkollegium till K.M:t, vol. 41, 10.10.1690. The king had absolute faith in C. Bonde (Roos, *Uppkomsten av Finlands militieboställen under indelningsverkets nyorganisation 1682–1700*, p. 324).

For the sake of comparison given here are the balances of the general ledgers of the provinces of Sweden proper (which often contained considerable amounts of other sums than tax arrears alone; these balances were of the same order or smaller than the annual expenditures of the provincial economy):

Table 8. Crown receivables in Swedish provinces

Örebro 1693	220,378	
Jönköping 1694	54,124	
Västernorrland 1694	169,781	silver dalers
Älvsborg 1699	136,803	
Östergötland 1703	195,775	
Västernorrland 1703	271,458	

Comparing these figures further with the province balances of the general ledgers of the realm for 1669 and 1677,[199] it can be seen that tax arrears did not in any way increase in Sweden to the degree that they did in Finland, although also there the restitution restored the peasants to crown taxation in precisely the same way as in Finland. The only possible conclusion from this is that the level of taxation laid down in the early 17th century in Sweden corresponded to the solvency of the peasants much better than in Finland. Crown taxation was at a realistic level in Sweden but far too high in Finland. The difference was probably due to the so-called minor ice age that had severe effects on the northern marginal areas of agriculture.[200]

---

[199] RA, Kammararkivet, Länsräkenskaper (the more or less random selection is due to the fact that most of the provincial accounts in the Swedish National Archives are not permitted for use). RA, Kammararkivet, Kammarkollegiet, Generalbokhålleriet, Rikshuvudbok 1669 & 1677 (KA, FR 1607 & 1604).

[200] I have no information on any other possible reasons. Despite crown taxation that functioned well in Sweden, the country's peasants were in considerable arrears in the late 17th century to their noble landlords and corporative holders of donations. Jan-ken Myrdal, *Jordbruket under feodalismen 1000–1700* (Borås, 1999), pp. 330–332;Thoré, *Akademibondens plikt, universitetets rätt*, pp. 217–234.

The crown lists of arrears distinguished hopeless arrears that would no longer be collected from cases for which there was still hope and where collection was still attempted. The lists of arrears make depressing reading. Aged, blind, disease-ridden peasants and their widows could not manage their farms and tax payments and had to beg for their sustenance as their arrears to the crown continued to grow.

In some cases the nobleman or holder of the office-related estate to which the peasant's taxes had been assigned had taken the last crust of bread and ruined the whole farm. For example, according to a list of arrears from 1676 regimental clerk Johan Schmidt had seized all that he could from one Thomas Mårtensson of Viikainen in Letala Parish without giving any receipt, as a result of which the latter had given notice and gone begging. At Tyllilä in S:t Mårtens local officers had driven a widow named Gertrud to ruin.

According to the same list from 1676, Henrik Matsson of Saari in Lappi Parish had been conscripted on account of arrears. Johan Jakobsson of Pikis lost his farm to the crown because of arrears, and in 1667 he served as a farmhand on his former property. The loss of hereditary rights, eviction and conscription were the most serious means used by the crown in combating arrears, but owing to the shortage of labour it would apply these measures only against the worst recalcitrants. At Jokioinen in Kangasala, one Johan Bengtsson had lost his hereditary rights and the master (presumably a nobleman) had seized everything that he could, which still did not pay the arrears in full, whereupon Johan could only pay a quarter of his arrears to the crown in 1670.

The poetic standard entry describing the penniless in the records was *"äger varken ko eller so"* ("owns neither cow nor sow"). One Mårten Jöransson of Hallu in Nykyrko was thus marked in the records for the year 1664 and owed the county the considerable sum of more than 700 silver dalers as well as 8 dalers to the crown. According to the lists there were those who did not even own a nail in the wall (thus having no fear of forced sale of property). According to the list of arrears for 1664, Sara Bertilsdotter

149

of Hyrkkölä village in Lembois was unable to pay a small amount of arrears and as a result a cooking pot was confiscated from her as collateral; another widow of Lembois forfeited livestock to the crown for the same reason. In 1670 it was noted that the arrears of Anders Korjus of Tavastkyro could not be collected as he had been beheaded the previous year, without leaving any inheritance at all.

Many peasants tried to cancel their arrears and start a new life elsewhere by escaping their holdings to other parts of Finland, or to Sweden, the Baltic lands or other parts. The crown bailiff was kept at bay by paying at least part of the tax debts. According to the lists of arrears, the fate of the aged, the infirm and widows was often bleak. At worst the poor could starve to death. According to the list of arrears for the year 1676, five persons died of hunger in the famine year of 1675 at the farm of Jakob Jakobsson, an indigent peasant of Seppälä village in Letala. At Töysälä in Vittis Påhl Jakobsson had died without leaving anything and his children begged. The lists of arrears were long, and poverty was truly widespread in both the towns and the countryside.[201]

Sometimes it was stated outright in the lists of arrears that unduly high taxes had ruined the farm in question.[202] The state of affairs was also known to the crown bailiffs.

Arrears and tax instalments did away with hereditary rights of peasants, and it became easy for the crown to evict and replace them with new farmers.[203] In practice, however, the vast majority

---

[201] Lists of arrears: KA, 7289 (1663), 7292 (1664), 7303 b (1667), 7314 a (1670), 7336 (1676), 7383 b (1689).

[202] KA, 7389 b, pp. 6464–6465.

[203] The king ordered the punishment of running the gauntlet to a peasant neglecting the care of his farm, but it was rarely enacted. KA, 6830, p. 309, Charles XI to L. Creutz 7.3.1691. In 1696 King Charles XI issued an order according to which the peasants of salary estates, auxiliary properties of cavalry-service estates and estates non-assigned to the military, who did not tend to their farms and responsibilities despite being urged to do so, could be evicted. The order does not make any mention of hereditary rights or district court proceedings. This order, too, was mainly a threat that could be applied to extreme cases for purposes of intimidation, and not any automatic consequence of neglect. KA, Karl XI:s registratur 1696 (avskrift), to L. Creutz 14.8.1696.

of the crown peasants were allowed, despite arrears, to keep their farms and to pass them on to their descendants. Owing to the shortage of labour, the crown could not afford large-scale evictions of peasants. Only those who neglected their farms and responsibilities the most were evicted and some were also enrolled in the army. They became cautionary examples for others. The accumulation of large arrears without any easement from the crown and the conflicts with the representatives of the crown that arose from their collection nonetheless led to uncertainty, dissatisfaction and restlessness, while also eroding general obedience to the law.

It was possible to buy back the hereditary rights by paying all of one's arrears. At one farm in Letala, they were first bought back from the crown and after being lost once again from the county.[204] The consequence of unduly high taxes was paid by the descendants of the 17th-century donated-land peasants in the following century, when family rights began to be bought back in large numbers.

KING CHARLES XI, THE CHAMBER COLLEGE AND ARREARS

As the restitution restored the tax revenue donated to the nobles back to the crown and arrears began to grow rapidly, the crown should have intervened speedily and lowered taxes, if the idea of the negotiating state and listening to the voice of the subjects were also true here. But what was the real state of affairs?

In early 1687, the above-mentioned inspector Mallenius of the admiralty officially informed on Creutz and Axel Rosenhane, the now resigned governor of the Province of Nyland and Tavastehus for the large arrears from Finland that were owed to the admiralty.

---

[204] KA, judicial district of Vemo and Lower Satakunta II, judgment book 1697, p. 571 (Letala autumn district court sessions 8.–9.11.1697).

The king, in whose autocratic hands the affairs of the realm were, was prone to think that the arrears were due to negligence and possible mismanagement on the part of crown officials, and by no means to any unduly high level of taxation.[205]

In 1693 King Charles XI paid attention to the balances of the South-Finnish provinces which had grown to truly large proportions and ordered the provincial governors to investigate the matter together with the Chamber College. In its reply to the king, the College observed that it had ordered the governors on several occasions since 1687 to devote their efforts to the collection of arrears. The organization of the allotment system, however, had taken up so much of the governors' time that they were in no way able to address the problem of arrears and balances. The Chamber College thus agreed to understand the problems of the governors but also let them know the king's opinion. The royal order dictated by Charles XI in to the letter from the Chamber College to the governors shows that he still regarded the arrears as resulting from negligence on the part of one or several persons. He believed that a considerable portion of the arrears could well be collected.[206]

At times the Chamber College and the king did understand the real background for the accumulation of arrears, but if one showed understanding towards those who had accumulated arrears the other would soon restore order. As described above, the Chamber College restored order in the matter of arrears due from the provinces of Ostrobothnia and Tavastehus, while now it was the king who rejected the Chamber College's view of understanding the position of the governors.

---

[205] RA, Kammarkollegium till K.M:t, vol. 32, 14.2. & 14.3.1687.
[206] RA, Kammarkollegium till K.M:t, vol. 51, 8.12.1693; KA, Karl XI:s registratur 1693 (avskrift), to the provincial governors of Finland 15.12.1693 and the Chamber College 19. and 24.10.1693 and registratur 1691, to several provincial governors 15. and 16.8.1691; RA, Landshövdingars skrivelser till K.M:t, Åbo och Björneborgs län, vol. 9, L. Creutz 12.9.1691, Nylands och Tavastehus län, vol. 3, A. Horn 18.10.1688 (KA, FR 43, 16) and other voluminous correspondence related to arrears in Finland.

THE AUTOCRACY OF KING CHARLES XI AND THE TAX-PAYING COMMONERS – CONCLUSIONS ON THE POWER STATE AND INTERACTION

In the long run the peasants benefited from the restitution implemented by Charles XI as it reduced the supremacy of the nobles and permitted the other estates to rise in power, but these benefits were not achieved until the decades after the Great Northern War. In the 17th century, the restitution did not improve the position of the peasants in any way. Under the authority of the crown, tax collection became more efficient, and the peasants were the party to suffer in those connections. While it lasted, the period of autocracy offered the peasants hardly any benefits.[207]

The district courts applied their right to participate in tax rulings by sanctioning the list of instalments of the current year (i.e. holdings that were abandoned [*öde*], taken under cultivation on the basis of tax exemption [*upptagna*], and ones that had reduced taxes [*förmedlade*]).[208] In this respect, we may well speak of interaction and even of a negotiating state, but we must also ask whether they were of any significance at this time. There is namely reason to underline that the core issue of taxation, unduly high taxes and the resulting immense arrears that accumulated after the restitution remained unresolved far too long and actually without any solution at all. After 1688 the crown began to grant easements of taxation through new levyings. This, however, was not enough, as the arrears and balances continued to grow. The implementation of the military tenure system (*det ständiga knektehållet*) and the crop failures and mass mortality of the

---

[207] Particularly in view of the fact that the benefits of military tenure system in comparison with hated and feared forced conscription were already lost in 1700 during the first year of the Great Northern War as the old measures were again resumed. Kujala, *Miekka ei laske leikkiä*, pp. 76–81. The autocracy of Charles XI also undermined the interests of the burghers and the clergy were put on a shorter leash than before. See Karonen, *Pohjoinen suurvalta*, pp. 305–306.

[208] Mäntylä, 'Kronan och undersåtarnas svält,' pp. 48–50.

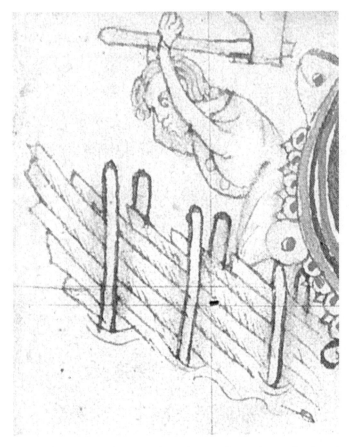

A peasant engaged in fence repair work according to the medieval work
Codex Aboensis. Helsinki University Library

mid-1690s forced the crown to reduce taxes even more, but as a quarter or a fifth of the population died, the measures of the crown necessarily remained insufficient. No doubt, taxation that was kept at an unnecessarily high level for decades did not fan the peasants' enthusiasm to fulfil their obligations. On the contrary, it eroded obedience to the law, which the crown would feel during the Great Northern War in the form of widespread disobedience.[209]

There is reason to note the paradox that despite arrears that grew to immense amounts and the process of reducing taxes that was implemented in the 1690s, the economy of the provinces of Åbo and Björneborg and Nyland and Tavastehus maintained a good ability to finance the operations necessary to the crown. The arrears for a single annual period were of a level that would not impair the finances of the province. It was only the accumulated total of arrears over a period of several years that was several times the annual volume of the provincial economy and it was impossible to collect this sum from the defaulters on a short time. Partly owing to this situation, the roots of the problem of immense accumulated arrears were not addressed in earnest.[210]

Even with reference solely to the period before 1695, we cannot reasonably come to any other conclusion except that the actual situation of the peasants was ignored. In other words, interaction at the level of crown taxation was realized highly imperfectly, or not at all. There is no reason to speak of any negotiating state in this connection. With regard to the crown and the tax reductions, the perspective of the power state that many scholars have so easily rejected, is quite arguable. On the other hand, in the relations between the nobles and their tenant farmers, the concept of interaction seems to work – an interaction of deeply unequal parties realized through contradictions and distorted by the severe discipline of the nobles and their subordinates, which nevertheless permitted even the weaker party to have some influence on matters, at least in Southwest Finland. I do not want to deny the justification of even the negotiating state, for, as is well known, the Swedish nobility was able to turn its weakness into strength by ceasing to pursue its interests to the letter and by recognizing

---

[209] On the developments and catastrophes of the 1690s see below.
[210] Kujala, *Miekka ei laske leikkiä*, pp. 53–55.

at least the insignificant rights of the peasants.[211] At issue here are different perspectives suited in different way to describing various aspects of society and also reflecting the overall views of society of those who present them. I would underscore conflicts within society rather than harmony that was realized in practice quite poorly, or upon the conditions of the stronger party.

The result is thus that in its ascendancy the crown during the autocracy of Charles XI took less account of the wishes of the peasants than the 17th-century nobility of Sweden, which was weak in comparison with its counterparts elsewhere. The other side of the coin should also be remembered, viz. that the high nobility of Sweden transferred considerable resources from their Finnish estates to themselves in Sweden without providing hardly any compensation for this tax revenue that was donated to them,[212] while autocracy directed the taxes that it had restituted to defence, which in principle benefited all of its subjects. The transfer of resources to the nobles that took place in the peak period of the donation system in the mid-17th century, was, however, possible only during an exceptional international situation, when Sweden's traditional enemies, Russia, Poland and Denmark, were weak. The weakness of the Swedish forces in the war with Denmark in the 1670s was a decisive catalyst towards the emergence of autocracy and restitution of tax revenue. When Russia broke out of isolation a couple of decades later to become a European

---

[211] Peter Englund, *Ofredsår* (Stockholm, 1993), pp. 504–518; also Karonen, *Pohjoinen suurvalta*, pp. 434–435.

[212] The same almost complete lack of compensation naturally applied also to tax revenue received by nobles from Sweden by way of donations. I find grounds to speak of almost complete lack of compensation, although I am aware that the generous donations made by Queen Christina at the turn of 1650s were a reward, in donation form, for the sacrifices and services provided by the nobility in the Thirty Years' War and were meant to bind them to the crown. The other form of donated taxes, the purchased or pledged donated estates belonged to their possessor on the basis of a direct economic transaction, purchase or a pledge in lieu of receivables. The lack of compensation for the donations becomes apparent in view of the improvements that crown could make to the armed forces and administration of the realm as the result of tax revenues regained through restitution.

power, Sweden was forced to use the resources of poor Finland on-site to secure the "curtain wall and larder" of Stockholm against the threat from the east.

In 17th-century Finland, taxation too high in relation to resources maintained a kind of hidden crisis of society that would emerge in times of war and crop failure. The crown and the nobility could ease matters in individual cases, but it was in the interest of neither party to address the actual causes of the problem, and on the other hand there were no distinct calls for change from below.

PROBLEMS FOR AUTOCRACY

POPULATION IN THE LATE 17TH CENTURY AND THE FAMINE YEARS OF 1696–1697

Table 9. The estimated population of the Kingdom of Sweden ca. 1700

Sweden	1,370,000
Finland	350,000
Province of Kexholm	30,000
The Baltic provinces	500,000
Territories conquered in Germany	1,000,000
Total	3,250,000

Source: Karonen, *Pohjoinen suurvalta*, p. 34

According to Oiva Turpeinen, the respective populations of Finland, the Province of Kexholm and the Baltic provinces (Ingermanland, Estonia and Livonia) were higher than the figures given by Karonen.[213] The latter figures in any case point to the size of the population in different parts of the realm. The population of Sweden can be compared with contemporary

---

[213]   Oiva Turpeinen, 'Suomen väestö 1636–1996 sekä vertailu Viroon.'

population of France, a veritable European power, which had 21 million inhabitants. In the year 1700, fourteen million people lived in the territory enclosed by the 1914 borders of the German Empire, a population figure also reached by Russia, Sweden's eastern neighbour. Poland, Sweden's other bordering neighbour, had a population of nine million. The population of Sweden, however, exceeded that of its third neighbour, Denmark-Norway, and also the population of Holland. In 1690 Denmark had approximately 650,000 inhabitants and the population of Norway was approximately 490–500,000. In 1700 Holland had a population of less than two million.[214]

In Finland and other parts of Northern Europe the harvests of 1695 and 1696 were exceptionally poor owing to cold weather and rain. Crop failure led to famine and the mass movement of large numbers of beggars, which also spread contagious diseases. According to Seppo Muroma, the population of Finland decreased by 27% between the end of 1695 and the beginning of 1698. Including the Province of Kexholm, the figure was 28 percent. At the end of 1695, Finland had a population of ca. 440,000; the corresponding figure at the beginning of 1698 was 323,000. Including the Province of Kexholm, population of the country decreased from 500,000 to 360,000.[215]

Muroma estimates the population of Finland according to its late 17th-century border with Sweden, which in Lapland followed a course further to the south and the east than at present. Turpeinen, in turn, makes reference to the border of 1812 (1809), which still exists between Sweden and Finland. According to him, the population of Finland, including the Province of Kexholm

214 *Histoire des populations de l'Europe*, Jean-Pierre Bardet & Jacques Dupâquier (eds) (Fayard, 1997), pp. 429, 449, 519, 557, 566; William C. Fuller Jr., *Strategy and Power in Russia, 1600–1914* (New York, 1992), p. 65; Knud J. V. Jespersen, *Danmarks historie*, 3 (København, 1989), p. 45; *Norges historie*, Knut Mykland (ed.), 7 (Oslo, 1977), p. 149; Rolf Danielsen et al., *Norway: A History from the Vikings to Our Own Times* (Oslo, 1995), p. 132.
215 Muroma, *Suurten kuolovuosien (1696–1697) väestönmenetys Suomessa*, pp. 179–180, 292.

was 556,400 at the end of 1695, and respectively 433,400 in early 1698, the loss thus amounting to 22%. Differences with regard to Muroma's estimates are mainly due to the fact that Turpeinen raises the estimates for the population of Karelia and the Province of Kexholm in particular. Mortality in the years 1696–1697 exceeded all the later demographic catastrophes of Finnish history many times over.[216] This was without doubt the most serious accident ever to befall the Finnish population.

At the beginning of the 18th century, the proportion of the nobility of the total population of Sweden and Finland was 0.5% and that of the clergy was 1 %. Less than 2 % of the population belonged to the estate of the burghers, but in addition to holders of burgher rights the towns included less affluent inhabitants. The category of so-called "non-noble persons of rank" (*ofrälse ståndspersoner*) consisted of the owners of estates, crown officials, entrepreneurs etc. (1–2%). The remaining 95% of the population consisted of the common people: peasants, the landless rural population and the poor inhabitants of the towns.[217]

THE ECONOMY OF THE REALM

In 1682 only 4.6% of the whole population of Finland lived in the town. At the beginning of the 18th century, Åbo had approximately 6,000 inhabitants and Viborg and Helsingfors each had a population between two and three thousand. The remaining towns of Finland were even smaller. Stockholm, the capital of the realm, had almost 60,000 inhabitants. In speaking of the economy of the realm one should not ignore the towns and burghers engaged in trade and commerce, through whom most of the country's agricultural produce was sold.[218]

---

216   Oiva Turpeinen, 'Suomen väestö 1636–1996 sekä vertailu Viroon'.
217   Sverker Oredsson, 'Karl XII', *Tsar Peter och kung Karl: Två härskare och deras folk* (Stockholm, 1998), pp. 37–39.
218   Mäntylä, 'Suurvaltakausi', pp. 247–256.

Sweden (including Finland) had a poor and backward agrarian economy. But the country had considerable income from the export of iron and copper. Mining and the export of its products was one of the cornerstones of Sweden's role as a leading European power. In 1685, the export of iron, steel, copper and brass accounted for 80% of the value of all Swedish exports. Pitch and tar accounted for 8 percent. The mining and metal industry concentrated mainly in Sweden, but the tar that was exported from the realm came predominantly from Ostrobothnia and Eastern Finland. Finland's share in the exports of the realm was as small as its proportion of the population of the kingdom. Tar was nonetheless one of the main strategic export products of the realm. Around the year 1700 England imported up to 80% of its bar iron and 85% of its tar from Sweden. The Royal Navy could not stay afloat without Finnish tar.[219]

In the 1690s the Baltic provinces of Estonia and Livonia in particular produced an annual surplus of several hundred thousand silver dalers, which was transferred to the royal treasury.[220] As noted above, the high nobility transferred significant resources from their properties in Finland to their own households in Sweden. Before restitution, the crown received such a small proportion of the tax revenue coming from Finland that it was hard put to make it cover local needs of administration and defence.

After restitution, the crown truly tried to transfer resources from Finland to the royal treasury in Stockholm. Accordingly, the

---

[219]   Sten Carlsson/Jerker Rosén, *Svensk historia*, I (Stockholm, 1964), pp. 677–678; Sven-Erik Åström, 'Suurvalta-ajan valtiontalous,' *Suomen taloushistoria*, I, pp. 294–299; Markku Kuisma, *Metsäteollisuuden maa: Suomi, metsät ja kansainvälinen järjestelmä 1620–1920* (Helsinki, 1993), pp. 23–39. The basic work on the economic history of the period is still Heckscher, *Sveriges ekonomiska historia från Gustav Vasa*, I:2. On the mining and metal industries, see Georg Haggrén, *Hammarsmeder, masugnsfolk och kolare: Tidigindustriella yrkesarbetare vid provinsbruk i 1600-talets Sverige* (Pieksämäki, 2001).

[220]   Walter Ahlström, *Arvid Horn och Karl XII 1710–1713* (Lund, 1959), p. 90; David Kirby, *Northern Europe in the Early Modern Period: The Baltic World 1492–1772* (London, 1993), p. 257.

Province of Åbo and Björneborg paid 31,506 dalers to the treasury, 7,233 dalers for the construction of the royal castle in Stockholm, and 2,318 silver dalers to the stores of the Stockholm castle in 1691. These transfers of funds amounted to approximately 15% of the annual expenditure of the province. In 1694, 1695 and 1699 the Stockholm treasury received approximately 40,000 dalers each year from the province. The Province of Nyland and Tavastehus forwarded 29,495 dalers in 1692, the Province of Viborg remitted 35,901 dalers in 1690 and the Province of Ostrobothnia paid in 8,261 dalers in 1695. In poor years, however, the flow of resources was reversed. It must be noted, however, that Stockholm tried to recover and collect at a later stage the assistance that had been paid out for crop failure. In any case, the transfer of tax revenue from Finland to Sweden even in the good years of the 1690s remained relatively limited and they can be regarded as corresponding in volume to the share of this part of the realm in maintaining the functions of its administrative centre without any reason to speak of any kind of colonialist relationship. After the outbreak of the Great Northern War, there were hardly any resources available from Finland to be transferred to Stockholm.[221] The flow of revenue was again reversed. The Swedish army in Finland was funded with considerable sums of money from Stockholm until the year 1709, after which also this flow of resources dried up following the Swedish defeat at Poltava.[222]

---

[221] The general ledgers of the provinces. Also Kujala, *Miekka ei laske leikkiä*, p. 57. I have not taken into account tax revenue directed towards the navy from Finland. In the 1690s they were paid in any considerably amounts only from the Province of Ostrobothnia, which was in compensation for the fact that this province maintained only a single regiment of infantry, i.e. it compensated for the navy the cost of maintaining a regiment of cavalry. Moreover, a considerable part of the taxes meant for the navy always remained in arrears in the province.

[222] Kujala, 'Why Did Finland's War Economy Collapse During the Great Northern War?', pp. 86–89.

THE TAX REDUCTIONS OF THE 1690S AND THE RAISING OF TAXES DURING THE GREAT NORTHERN WAR

In my previous publications in both English and Finnish I have discussed the tax reductions of the 1690s and the new war taxes or contributions introduced by King Charles XII (1697–1718) on the eve of the Great Northern War (1700–1721) and at the beginning of the war. Here, I repeat only the most important points without evidence in the form of tables. In 1688 the crown began to revise the taxation of the peasants of the Province of Åbo and Björneborg through new levyings. Measures applied by the crown included reductions of taxes (*förmedling*) and in the late 1690s partial repeal of taxes (*avskattning*). A considerable portion of the peasants (farms) of the provinces of Åbo and Björneborg and Nyland and Tavastehus were granted reduction in taxation, because this was required by the functioning of the allotment system. The crown had to reduce taxes in order to make it possible for the farms paying their taxes to soldiers and crown officials to manage them. Unduly high taxation led to arrears and inability to pay taxes, and a situation in which the holders of properties and benefices receiving tax revenue were left without income. There were attempts to make the system as stable and permanent as possible, with each recipient of taxed income always receiving the salary that was laid down and could be expected. This system could not tolerate any disturbances. In practice, however, the allotment system never functioned without disturbances, and could never be completely established, as had been the ideal. With the above mentioned repeals of taxation, the crown sought to alleviate the demographic and economic catastrophe caused by the total crop failures of the 1690s and unprecedented mass mortality, being however unable to succeed in this impossible task.

The new policy could not halt the growth of arrears in the provinces of Finland except temporarily in the early 1690s in the Province of Nyland and Tavastehus, which was apparently an indication of personal favour from King Charles XI to Governor C. Bonde of the province, as has been stated previously. The reductions were thus mostly insufficient and they were not actually carried out to ease the situation of the peasants but to serve the crown's own interests.

Anticipating problems, the crown began in 1699 to collect contributions in addition to regular taxes. In the following year, war broke out between Sweden and its neighbours, Denmark, Poland (more precisely Poland's King August II of Saxony) and Russia, all of which wanted to recover territories taken from them by Sweden.

Comparing the tax reductions of the 1690s with the increases now provided by the contributions in the Province of Åbo and Björneborg, it can be seen that the former reduction was roughly equivalent to slightly over half or two thirds of the increase caused by the contributions. From 1700 onwards taxation remained in principle at the same level until 1713, when the massive Russian invasion of Finland also prevented regular tax collection. Exceptions were the years 1704 and 1710, when larger amounts of contributions were collected than normally.[223] In the longer term, the increase in taxation was between over one tenth and less than one fifth and not 20% as claimed in earlier Finnish studies. The same situation presumably applied also in the Province of Nyland and Tavastehus, although the loss of the province's general ledgers for the turn of the 17th and 18th centuries impedes further study of the matter. Nonetheless, claims of a general increase of taxation are misleading. We must take a closer look at which groups paid more taxes than previously after the turn of the century.

After the year 1700 the military contributions had not increased the taxation of the common rural populace any more than its tax burden had been reduced in the previous decade. The increase

---

[223]   In 1704 the contributions were collected in double amounts, but the temporary raise of 1710 applied only to other estates than the peasants.

in taxation thus had to be paid by completely other estates than the peasants. On the other hand, the contributions from the nobility were no doubt ultimately paid by their peasants, which placed the peasants appended to the nobility in a worse position than those who paid their taxes to the crown, even despite the fact that the former would pay the contribution of rural populace at a rate per *mantal* unit that was only half of that required from the rest of the rural commoners.

It must also be kept in mind that only some of the farms were awarded tax reductions in the 1690s. The peasants whose taxes had not been alleviated now had to pay new contributions without having received any corresponding reduction in taxes at an earlier stage. Despite everything the increase in the tax burden applied more to the nobles, clergy, burghers and civil servants than the peasants.

On the other hand, in the longer term, the conscription of males for war service made it necessary to produce the same or slightly risen taxes with a smaller workforce than before, and in this sense also the tax burden of the peasants rose without doubt. In the year 1700 some 24,000 soldiers were conscripted from Finland, the total rising to almost 50,000 for the duration of the Great Northern War, which led to a shortage of labour particularly at the beginning of the war. Conscripted troops numbering 24,000 and 50,000 were a sizeable deduction from a total population of some 400,000 Finns, also in view of the fact that possibly ca. 43,000 of them were lost in the war. The total number of civilian casualties of the Great Northern War in Finland was only 11,000, which is quite small in view of the dismal picture that prevails of the Russian occupation of Finland in the years 1713–1721. It must be pointed out, however, that all the above figures are only estimates.

Except for the years 1704 and 1710, the level of taxation remained constant from 1700 until 1712. It was measured above with the sums of levied taxes given in the general provincial ledgers from which instalments i.e. tax exemption granted because of tax donation or officially noted inability to pay taxes were deduced. On the other hand, the taxes to be collected for each year include the arrears for that year, i.e. taxes left unpaid without due permission. The crown receivables as a whole give an idea of the arrears (at least in Finland), as was done previously in this book. It is, however, extremely laborious and almost impossible to read from the accounts what portion of the taxes of a specific year actually remained unpaid, as the arrears were gradually paid off over the course of several years. We may therefore ask whether figures of annually collected taxes actually show that the tax burden remained quite stable. It is quite commonly held that owing to the distress caused by the war, tax arrears grew and the crown economy was caught in a vicious circle of diminishing revenue. This idea was already formulated in the 19th century by the Swedish scholar G. E. Axelson. The suggestion of the war causing pauperization on a large scale was already questioned in Swedish studies in the early 1900s, but this idea has influenced thinking in Finland until quite recently.

The proportion of arrears in relation to collected taxes and their possible growth can be viewed with reference to funds used annually by the crown (in this case the Province of Åbo and Björneborg) for provincial salaries, war expenses, administration etc. The question is whether or not they remained more or less the same throughout the war or did they possibly diminish year by year. The funds used by the crown, or annual expenditure (with the title *anordningarna* in the general ledgers) include taxes channeled into salaries through the allotment system, which were not collected by the crown. The collection was left by the correction to those who held the posts. The crown, nonetheless, benefited from these taxes through the work of officials and soldiers.

Diagram 2 given here shows that in the Province of Åbo and Björneborg annual crown expenses in the period 1700–1712 varied more than the collected taxes, but there is no cause to speak of any continually descending or spiraling trend even in the first-mentioned case. The economy of the Province of Åbo and Björneborg did not shrink by any means because of the war but

Diagram 2. Crown taxes and expenditure in the Province of Åbo and Björneborg.

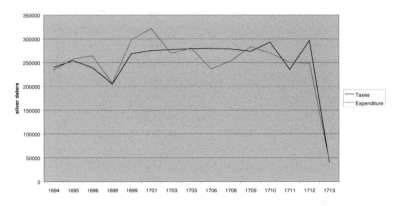

Source: General ledgers of the provincial accounts.

remained at a relatively stable level. The proportion of arrears in relation to collected taxes, the unknown quantity contained in the latter, varied according to the crops, but nonetheless remained relatively constant. Despite arrears and their increase, the provincial economy remained viable.

Table 10. The debet balance or crown receivables of the main calculation of the accounts of the Province of Åbo and Björneborg during the Great Northern War (according to the general ledgers)

	silver dalers
1700	853,322
1701	749,251
1703	689,130
1705	760,338
1710	851,667
1712	908,403

At the beginning of the war the crown cancelled large amounts of its own receivables, no doubt mostly arrears that were impossible to collect, and as a result the crown's receivables decreased until 1703. From then onwards, arrears and crown receivables began to grow again just as in the late 1680s and in the 1690s. Most of the receivables were taxes owed in arrears by peasants in the Province of Åbo and Björneborg and in Finland in general. No one can tell how much this was due to insolvency and how much to unwillingness, but despite arrears the system of paying taxes functioned quite well until 1713.

Exactly the same paradoxical situation prevailed during the war as before. Arrears continued to accumulate and their total exceeded the annual expenditure of the province many times over, but the annual arrears were nonetheless such a small portion of the income of the province economy that finances of the province remained viable and at a relatively stable volume up until the end of 1712. The arrears were the nightmare of the province treasurer and their total was such that collection in full was not possible in any conceivable period, or at all, but despite this the system remained surprisingly functional.[224]

In 1711 the government agreed to write off all the arrears accumulated by peasants up until the end of 1707, albeit only for taxes outside the allotment system, i.e. reserved solely for the crown (the arrears of which being the only ones recorded by the crown) and not revenue for the salaries of officials. In the accounts of the Province of Åbo and Björneborg, these cancelled arrears

---

[224] Kujala, *Miekka ei laske leikkiä*, pp. 46–55; Kujala, 'Why Did Finland's War Economy Collapse During the Great Northern War?', pp. 78–84. It should be noted that in the Province of Åbo and Björneborg, the crown had a small amount of other revenue than taxes and this income is not included in amounts of annual crown taxes given in Diagram 2. Figures related to the armed forces: Risto Valpas, *Länsi-Suomen väestöolot suurista kuolovuosista Uudenkaupungin rauhaan (1698–1721)*, unpublished licentiate study in Finnish and Scandinavian history, University of Helsinki 1965, p. 176. On pauperization: Gustaf Edvard Axelson, *Bidrag till kännedomen om Sveriges tillstånd på Karl XII:s tid* (Visby, 1888).

did not disappear in any way, but naturally there could no longer be attempts to collect them.[225]

The material that I have sampled from the upper administrative district of Hollola shows that the crown bailiffs and tax clerks were often quite successful in the partial collection of arrears – as is known they had a series of effective means at their disposal – but there was no power so great in the realm that it could have collected all the arrears due to the crown.

One of the means of coercion was, as mentioned above, the procedure whereby unpaid arrears would make a tax peasant lose his hereditary rights to the crown and became a so-called crown peasant who could easily be evicted from his property of necessary. This, however, was not generally done in Tavastia during the war years, possibly because of more efficient sanctions, above all the forced conscription of a peasant neglecting the payment of taxes. Not only a threat, these means were also applied.[226] On the basis of efficient sanctions and the functioning of the tax-paying system it can be estimated that the peasants left crown taxes unpaid only under pressing circumstances, i.e. insolvency was more widespread than mere unwillingness to pay.

THE ECONOMIC POSITION OF THE PEASANTS 1694–1713

In many recent studies, the number of abandoned farms and *mantal* units in relation to all farms and *mantal* units has been

[225] RA, Rådets registratur, 1711 maj-juli (Turun maakunta-arkisto [Turku Provincial Archives], RR 316), pp. 328–333, to the provincial governors 16.6.1711; Historiska handlingar, 5 (Stockholm, 1866), p. 107, 7 1870, pp. 169–173; KA, Karl XII:s registratur 1711 (avskrift), to the governors 8.1.1711. On the other hand, the partial remission of arrears declared by the government was taken into account in the general ledgers of the provinces of Nyland and Tavastehus and Ostrobothnia. KA, 8127, pp. 29, 361–366, 9261, pp. 13, 610–611.

[226] Jutikkala, 'Väestö ja yhteiskunta,' pp. 364–367, 385; Y. S. Koskimies, 'Suuren Pohjan sodan ja isonvihan aika,' Hämeen historia, II:2 1960, pp. 618–627, 644–650.

Fishing on the River Torne in the 16ᵗʰ century according to Olaus Magnus. Fishing was an important means of livelihood in all other rivers, as well. The crown and the nobility saw that they had their share too.

observed to be quite a good indication of the economic status of the peasants.[227] During the famine years of 1696–1697, the term not only meant a farm unable to pay taxes and for the most part uncultivated but where its residents still stayed, but also literally a farm where all the inhabitants had died.[228] In order to ensure its tax revenue, the crow quickly sought to resettle the abandoned farms, usually by granting temporary tax exemption for the new residents.[229] In areas where the proportion of abandoned farms and *mantal* units remained high after 1697, or even grew at a later stage, were in particularly deep economic and demographic crisis.

After the most part of tax revenue had returned to the crown in the restitution, the proportion of abandoned farms and *mantal*

227 E.g. Virrankoski, 'Pohjois-Pohjanmaa ja Lappi 1600-luvulla,' pp. 48–69; Mäntylä, *Kruunu ja alamaisten nälkä*.
228 Jutikkala, *Bonden i Finland genom tiderna*, pp. 208–212; Mäntylä, *Kruunu ja alamaisten nälkä*, pp. 10–14, 95–99.
229 Mäntylä, *Kruunu ja alamaisten nälkä*, pp. 17–24.

units was a better indication of the relative economic situation in a region than in the decades after the middle of the 17th century that were dominated by tax donations. At that stage certain areas of the economically relatively developed west coast had the highest figures for abandoned farms and *mantal* units. Despite this it is still necessary to take into account various local factors which increased the number of abandoned holdings and varied among regions. The following discussion seeks to outline how well the peasants survived the famine years and the effects of the war. The discussion also seeks to go from cameral reality to the world of the real economy, whose parameters also had to be taken into account in taxation.

Mortality in the years 1696–1697 was most severe among the landless population beneath the peasantry. The means of livelihood and stores of food of the former group were the most restricted and smallest and, more often than the holders of farms, they had to leave their homes and go begging with the resulting risk of dying from epidemics. Many farmers no doubt dismissed their hired hands when the stores of food began to dwindle, and the latter had no choice than to go begging. Also, small farms were abandoned more often than large ones. Death did not affect all groups in the same way.[230] Between 1696 and 1698, 27% of all farm holders (i.e. heads of households) in Finland-Proper had changed. The corresponding figure for Satakunta was 38% and as high as 44% for Ostrobothnia. This shows that even the farm holders were not spared.[231]

In Northern Ostrobothnia the proportion of abandoned farms in 1698 varied between 10 and over 20%, being as high 35% on the island of Karlö off Uleåborg. The figure for Central Ostrobothnia was ca. 10%, but in Southern Ostrobothnia, except for two or three parishes, there were hardly any abandoned farms despite a loss of a quarter of the population. The relatively high

---

230 Mäntylä, *Kruunu ja alamaisten nälkä*, pp. 63–70.
231 Muroma, *Suurten kuolovuosien (1696–1697) väestönmenetys Suomessa*, pp. 152–154.

mortality rate in Ostrobothnia correlated with abandonment in the north but not in the south. The abandoned farms were soon resettled in areas where the farming population had profitable auxiliary means of livelihood, such as tar burning in Southern and Central Ostrobothnia, and shipbuilding and fishing in the coastal parishes.

The crisis was worst in the areas that were dependent solely on farming and particularly on slash-and-burn agriculture. Flooding prevented fishing in the salmon rivers of Northern Ostrobothnia during the most severe shortage of food in the spring of 1696. The number of abandoned farms decreased quite slowly in the northern parts of the province after the great famine years. In other words, the economy did not recover in the same way as in Southern Ostrobothnia.

Only one regiment of troops was recruited from the Province of Ostrobothnia. Even with regard to later replacements, the province provided a relatively smaller number of soldiers than the three provinces of Southern Finland, each of which maintained three regiments and provided additional military contingents at the beginning of the war. Measured in terms of all instalments and particularly with regard to the numbers of abandoned farms, the economic status of the province improved especially in Southern Ostrobothnia, but also elsewhere. The crop failure of 1708–1709 had severe effects on the Province of Ostrobothnia, and together with the growing burden of the war it put agriculture in the province in a downward spiral. On the other hand, the degree of abandonment in Northern Ostrobothnia at the end of the decade and in the early 1710s was not as high as in the late 1690s, but the crisis was not basically alleviated until the Russian occupied the province in 1714. Southern Ostrobothnia, in turn, suffered only a small degree of abandonment and the first signs of an improving economy could already be seen there in 1712.[232]

---

[232]   Mäntylä, *Kruunu ja alamaisten nälkä*, pp. 60–70, 79–109, on war-time livelihoods and occupations in Ostrobothnia, see the accounts of province histories.

According to Lorentz Clerk, governor of the Province of Ostrobothnia, the economy of the province in the early 1710s was largely dependent on sealing, hunting and sea faring, because agriculture did not produce enough for sustenance, let alone taxes, and shipbuilding and tar burning were only bleak version of their former state. As was typical of the period, the governor's complaint was somewhat exaggerated, but its core points were nonetheless true. The most important point of his message to the Privy Council in Stockholm, however, was the recession of the traditional means of livelihood in Ostrobothnia, tar burning and shipbuilding.[233]

The recession of tar burning in Ostrobothnia and the tar trade in the whole Swedish realm in 1710–1711 resulted from the fact that in late 1709 Denmark had resumed hostilities with Sweden. Disturbances in shipping continued into the year 1711. Nevertheless, Sweden was able to restore its tar trade by 1713 to its pre-1710 levels.[234] This benefited both Ostrobothnia and its mercantile means of livelihood just before the province became a theatre of war and most of it was occupied by a foreign power.

In the northeastern parts of Finland-Proper (the administrative districts of Vemo, Virmo and Masku) approximately 10% of all farms were abandoned in 1697, but in the southeast, in the districts of Pikis and Halikko and in Lower Satakunta on the coast, the figures were even lower. Crop failure was of less extent than the average in the fertile farmlands of Finland-Proper and Lower Satakunta, and there were also maritime means of livelihood that eased the situation (fishing and peasant seafaring). On the other hand, the percentage of abandoned farms in the inland region of

---

[233] RA, Landshövdingars skrivelser till K.M:t, Österbottens län, vol. 7 (KA, FR 63), L. Clerk to the Privy Council 10.10.1710, 7.3. and 29.7.1711 and 16.7.1712.

[234] Sven-Erik Åström, *From Stockholm to St. Petersburg: Commercial Factors in the Political Relations between England and Sweden 1675–1700* (Helsinki, 1962), pp. 127–128; David Kirby, 'The Royal Navy's Quest for Pitch and Tar during the Reign of Queen Anne,' *Scandinavian Economic History Review* 1974, pp. 112–113; Kuisma, *Metsäteollisuuden maa*, pp. 38–41.

Upper Satakunta rose in the late 1690s and at the beginning of the following decade at worst to over 18. Here, the crisis of agriculture was just as bad as in Northern Ostrobothnia.

The slight recovery of agriculture in the Province of Åbo and Björneborg ended with the outbreak of war in 1700. Large-scale recruitment of troops led to a severe shortage of labour. The course of development could be described as the stagnation of a crisis. The crop failures of 1704–1709, of which 1708 was the worst, raised the proportion of abandoned farms out of all holdings in Finland-Proper and Lower Satakunta to almost ten per cent and to ca. 15% in Upper Satakunta in 1709 or 1710. The crisis of agriculture was, however, now less severe than over ten years previously except in the administrative districts of Pikis, Halikko and Lower Satakunta, which had fared quite well in the crop failures of the 1690s.

Better crops than before were obtained from 1710 onwards, which was reflected in decreasing numbers of abandoned farms in 1710 or by 1712 at the latest. A particularly good crop was obtained in 1713, and when the Russians were advancing towards the end of the year into the Province of Åbo and Björneborg distress was being alleviated. Improved tax-paying ability and economic conditions in the countryside in the Province of Åbo and Björneborg during the last years is a surprise in view of the opposite trend in Ostrobothnia, but it can be seen before long that developments in the Province of Nyland and Tavastehus followed the same course as that the Province of Åbo and Björneborg. Ths also refutes the long-standing conception that the whole country deteriorated in an ever deeper direction during the war years.

In 1697 the proportion of abandoned farms of all holdings in Tavastia was at least over one-tenth, and perhaps as high as one fourth in the environs of Tavastehus. In Tavastia, the large drop in population coincided with large numbers of abandoned farms. In Nyland the economic crisis of the late 1690s was of the same order as in Finland-Proper, being more severe in East Nyland than in the western parts of the province. Also on the coast of

Nyland, maritime means of livelihood provided suitable sustenance.

Economic development in the Province of Nyland and Tavastehus during the war was similar that that of its neighbouring western province. The number of abandoned farms began to decrease and the economy began to improve by 1712 at the latest. Around 1710–1711 both Nyland and Tavastia, with the exception of the latter's northeastern part, had approximately a 10% abandoned farm rate, which means that the level was somewhat higher than in Finland-Proper.

A special feature of the Province of Nyland and Tavastehus was that the eastern and northeastern parts of Tavastia recovered – in numbers of abandoned farms – quickly from the crop failures of the late 1690s and the early 1700s and except for the crop-failure years they generally had quite small numbers of abandoned farms and *mantal* units. The province was thus the opposite mirror image of the Province of Åbo and Björneborg; in the latter province abandonment was worst in the interior parts of Upper Satakunta, while in Tavastia the inland periphery survived exceptionally well. The reason for this was the existence of substitutive means of livelihood: inland fishing, hunting and tar burning. As pointed in Table 3 above, Upper Satakunta still had a relatively small number of abandoned *mantal* units in the second half of the 17th century. The famine years thus forced this area into a deep economic crisis.

Of all the *mantal* units in the Province of Åbo and Björneborg, with the exception of Åland, 8.1% were abandoned in 1709. In 1710, 8.3% of the total number of *mantal* units in the Province of Nyland and Tavastehus were abandoned. The degree of abandonment was generally less severe when calculated in *mantal* units than in numbers of holdings, because the properties with low *mantal*-unit figures, i.e. with small yields paying taxes fell into an abandoned state more easily than the larger farms.[235]

---

235   Kujala, *Miekka ei laske leikkiä*, pp. 63–66 and the studies and sources mentioned in note 70 therein.

It is obvious that if the burden of war weighed more heavily in the provinces of Åbo and Björneborg and Nyland and Tavastehus than in Ostrobothnia during the first years of the war, the crop failures of 1708–1709, which were combined with disturbances in the tar trade, had a longer effect in the northernmost marginal areas of agriculture.

The large-scale recruitments of troops in the autumn of 1710 were facilitated by the fact that limited conscription in the preceding years had produced a reserve of potential troops, at least in Finland-Proper. On the other, it was possible to assemble only two-thirds of the planned number troops in Satakunta. This shows that an acute shortage of labour particularly applied to the problem province of Satakunta, where abandonment was also at a higher level than in Finland-Proper.

In 1703–1712 the Province of Åbo and Björneborg lost a proportionately greater number of farmhands than the provinces of Nyland and Tavastehus and Ostrobothnia, but with regard to hired labour in 1712 it was still slightly better placed than the Province of Nyland and Tavastehus, particularly if we take into account the numbers of women servants. In Satakunta there was a greater shortage of farmhands than in Finland-Proper. Most of this reduction in farmhands was presumably due to conscription.

The civilian population apparently increased throughout the war until the Russian occupation. The sending of farmhands and the landless population to war undermined the supply of labour, but population growth had the opposite effect. The farmers were helped by under-age boys and those among their adult relatives who were too old or physically unable to serve in the army.[236] Moreover, the contribution of wives, daughters and female servants was of prime importance for the survival of agriculture.[237] The farms thus did not have good conditions for practising agriculture

---

[236] Valpas, *Länsi-Suomen väestöolot suurista kuolovuosista Uudenkaupungin rauhaan (1698–1721)*, pp. 123–125, 190, 198–209.

[237] Jan Lindegren, 'Karl XII,' *Kungar och krigare* (Stockholm, 1993), p. 180.

and they were deteriorating, but the population was apparently able to adapt relatively well to the situation, and after weather conditions improved after 1710 the peasants were even able to improve their position. Improved crop yields without the crown trying to expropriate the resulting benefits by raising taxation could only benefit the peasants of Southwest Finland.

In the southeastern Karelian parts of the Province of Viborg an average up to 25% of all farms were insolvent and registered abandoned in 1700, while the corresponding figure in Savolax was only 8%. Viborg Karelia and the Province of Kexholm were a worse crisis area than even Northern Ostrobothnia. In 1708 only 7% of all farms in Savolax were listed abandoned. The relatively low degree of conscription in the Province of Viborg and the income provided by tar burning explain why Savolax was one of the regions of Finland that emerged best from this situation.

It took only four years (1712) for as many as 18% of the farms in Savolax to become abandoned. The deterioration of the situation in Savolax was above all due to the loss of the town of Viborg to Russia and the temporary halt of the tar trade caused by Denmark. Particularly in Savolax and Ostrobothnia, tar-burning was the main livelihood in providing the peasant with the cash to pay taxes.[238]

Savolax before 1709–1710 shows how even agriculture based on swidden methods could survive crop failure and war quite well if it had the support of profitable auxiliary means of livelihood.

Southern Ostrobothnia in particular, but also Northeast Tavastia, Finland-Proper and Nyland, survived the crop failures of 1696–1697 and 1704–1709 quite well in financial terms. Crop failure caused great economic losses in the parts of Karelia belonging to the Province of Viborg, the Province of Kexholm, Northern Ostrobothnia and Upper Satakunta, which did not have sufficient

---

[238]   Raino Ranta, *Viipurin komendanttikunta 1710–1721: Valtaus, hallinto ja oikeudenhoito* (Helsinki, 1987), pp. 447–449; Kujala, *Miekka ei laske leikkiä*, pp. 66–68 and quoted sources.

Making tar in a special tar-burning pit according to a drawing dating back to the mid-18th century. The Finnish word "tervahauta" (tar grave) has led the drawer to add a cross on the pit, contrary to the actual fact. The peasants of Ostrobothnia and Savolax earned the money needed for taxes by making tar. Helsinki University Library.

auxiliary livelihoods as buffers. Agriculture in the provinces of Åbo and Björneborg and Nyland and Tavastehus recovered in the early 1710s as weather conditions improved and it adapted surprisingly well to the effects of the war. On the other hand, Savolax and Ostrobothnia, which were dependent on foreign trade found themselves in worse economic problems than previously. Crop failures caused by nature were a worse scourge for the peasant than war, at least so long as the enemy remained beyond the borders.

The peasants of Southwest Finland thus survived the burdens of the war quite well. It is difficult to regard them solely as the involuntary objects of the power state who were unable to improve their own position. The same was noted above regarding the inhabitants of the County of Vasaborg in the 1660s–1680s. They maintained their own "grey economy" amidst the high numbers of abandoned farms. The crown of course was able to influence in essential ways the conditions under which the peasants operated and to even make their position difficult in decisive ways. After restitution, the crown forced the peasants of Vasaborg to an increasing degree to become farmers and more regular tax-payers than before. Natural catastrophes and external disturbances (war, obstacles to trade) could temporarily put the peasants on the brink of ruin.

The above, however, raises the question of why the crown did not take its own share of the affluence of the peasants of Southwestern Finland that had slightly grown in the early 1710s.

THE CRISIS OF AUTOCRACY

Having consolidated its position, autocracy under Charles XI was able to carry out restitution against the will of the majority of the nobility, the leading estate in society. At the same time, the king could afford to disregard the wishes of peasantry regarding the improvement of their own status. He adapted their taxes to suit the needs of the allotment system better without devoting any more time even to this class. The power state acted and society obeyed.

179

Stockholm, the capital of the kingdom in the late 17th century. The townscape is dominated by the old Royal Castle and its tower Tre Kronor (Three Crowns). The castle was badly destroyed by the fire of 7 May 1697. King Charles XI had got stomach cancer and died only a month earlier, on 5 April, at the age of 41. His body was still in the castle, and had to be evacuated as the fire broke out. The death of an autocratic ruler tends to leave the subjects perplexed and powerless, and the destruction of the castle did not improve the general spirit. Many people thought that the repeated misfortunes were an omen of future disasters. From Erik Dahlberg's illustrated work *Suecia antiqua et hodierna*. National Board of Antiquities.

The autocracy of Charles XI functioned as a mediator and referee between the estates. The allotment system ensured quite stable salaried income for the crown-service nobility, while the military tenure system, or regular maintenance of soldiers, exempted peasants from the hated levying of troops. At the same time, peasants under the authority of the nobility lost their former favoured position that was lighter by half than that of others in terms of conscription. The king's successful foreign policy kept Sweden out of wars for two decades, which could only spell great benefits for society.[239]

During the reign of Charles XII autocracy found itself in crisis and in part almost ceased to exist.[240] Conducting war abroad, the

---

[239] Upton, *Charles XI and Swedish Absolutism*.

[240] This is not to deny in any way that Sweden could still wage a debilitating war for years. This was made above all possible by the system created by King Charles XI (the allotment system securing the army and the state economy), but over time resources continued to dwindle. We cannot, however, speak of any functioning autocracy, as the Privy Council, the king's closest body of advisers, actively worked behind the scenes against the aims of the monarch, not to mention all the other crisis phenomena to be discussed below.

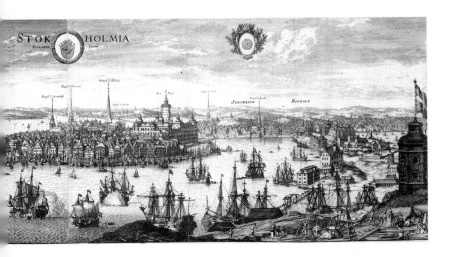

king did his utmost to prevent power from concentrating in single or few hands both in Stockholm and in various parts of the realm. He left his Privy Council without any real authority to lead, and when the council after the crushing defeat at Poltava in 1709 began to take responsibility for manage affairs in Sweden, it came into irreconcilable conflict with the king regarding the appropriateness of continuing the war, a course of action that Charles, seeking to restore his glory as a victorious military commander and to be compensated for Poltava, did not question for a moment. In this matter, the council, which disagreed with the king, interpreted the will of not only its own reference group, the high nobility, but also that of society at large.

The war did not give any group in society any new benefits; on the contrary it removed them – one after another – from both the high and low classes. Waging war far away and with poor communications, the king could not lead the country according to the needs of the situation, but neither did he permit the council to take control. This along with disagreement over the continuation of the war partly paralyzed the highest authority of the land.

When it was not used consistently to promote the military campaign, it resulted in a kind of vacuum of power that gave local officials greater leeway. The provincial governors of Finland, for example, began to keep a closer watch on the financial basis of their local power, the functioning of taxation, and partly on the interests of the inhabitants than on promoting the war effort. In fear of difficulties with the local populace they protected their ability to pay taxes against the demands of the army. They would seize without a moment's hesitation what they thought the populace could supply, but they were wary of straining the situation too much. Therefore, the Swedish army in Finland could not reap its share of the improved crops of the Southwest Finnish peasants in the early 1710. Competition among the provincial governors greatly impeded the war against Russia that was being fought on Finland's eastern border.

The army in Finland had in practice received tax funds for its use beyond the amount of contributions. The revenue came in form of auxiliary war taxes collected in advance, which were refunded to the tax payers in their final assessment of taxes. Following the way of thought typical of Swedish estate society, the rights and obligations of all groups were to correspond to each other. Social justice and predictability were realized when the rights of everyone were placed at a certain level – with regard to taxes naturally according to the cadastre. Accordingly, the principle of recompensing the auxiliary war taxes was completely natural not only for the governors but also for the Privy Council and the Budget Office (*Statskontoret*). But this prevented the army from benefiting from the improved crops. By beginning to keep control of the congruence of the auxiliary war taxes and the final taxes, the governors kept the army out of the peasants' grain stores.

Through new taxes and encumbrances, the war caused economic losses to other estates than the peasants alone. The obvious unwillingness of the clergy, civil servants and burghers to participate in the war effort with personal sacrifices was an example to the common people and was eagerly followed. Each

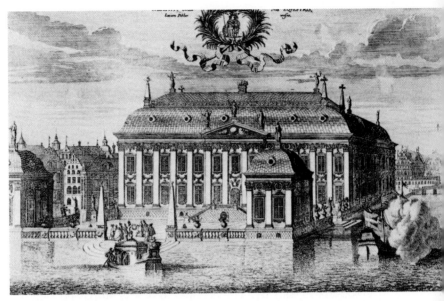

The House of the Nobility in Stockholm, second half of the 17th century, by architect Simon de la Vallée, meeting place of the estate of the nobility between 1668–1865. During Sweden's period of dominion, the nobility was divided into three classes, I) the titled nobility, i.e., the counts and barons; II) the knights, i.e., the heirs of the privy councillors; and III) the rest of the untitled nobility. In the votes within the estate, the House of the Nobility voted by class, not by head, so that the high nobility (the magnate families) in classes I and II could generally dominate the estate. In the Sweden of Charles XI and XII, the Swedish nobility was still the leading estate in society, although the autocracy had undermined its political influence. Restitution had derived the nobility of most of its new donations, leaving it with the old donations and a large number of manors which they managed under old conditions, with the exception of the new liability to provide for horsemen. Restitution had ensured the office-holding nobility more regular earnings. During the Great Northern War, the Crown was not able to pay the salaries either regularly or in full. The crown also charged the nobility with increasing new contributions and liabilities. War fatigue and the desire for peace started to gain ground, even among the king's own councilmen but the war-minded king would not hear of such ideas. National Board of Antiquities.

estate and section of the crown administration sought to safeguard its gains and benefits as closely as possible. The estates, areas of administration and crown officials all defended their own niches and territories with no consideration for the context as a whole or for joint interests. Nor did any cooperation emerge in these conditions between the peasants and the upper classes, even though they were active in the same direction in many issues. The king in turn promoted the lack of any kind of consensus with his negative position on matters such as convening the *Riksdag*. The autocracy of King Charles sought to atomize society to prevent the emergence of competing centres.[241]

Figures from the period 1620–1711 on convictions passed by district courts in the administrative district of Borgå on failure to meet obligations show that the first decade of the 18th century (1701–1710) with 616 convictions was one of the peak periods of subordination at the time. It was at the same level as the 1660s (1660–1669, with 647 convictions) and was surpassed only by the 1620s (1621–1630) with 1,001 convictions. All the other decades of the 17th century were much more peaceful.[242]

---

[241] These points are all discussed in closer detail in my book *Miekka ei laske leikkiä* (with an English summary) and in my article 'The Breakdown of a Society: Finland in the Great Northern War 1700–1714', *Scandinavian Journal of History* 2000, pp. 69–86.

[242] For the period 1621–1700, see Seppo Aalto, *Kirkko ja kruunu siveellisyyden vartijoina: Seksuaalirikollisuus, esivalta ja yhteisö Porvoon kihlakunnassa 1621–1700* (Helsinki, 1996), pp. 51–52, 227, and for the period 1701–1711, Kujala, *Miekka ei laske leikkiä*, pp. 88–90. In the administrative district of Jäskis in the Province of Viborg the largest number of convictions for insubordination (fines) fell into the ten-year periods 1661–1670 (546) and 1672–1682 (506). The eight-year period of the Great Northern War from which judgment books survive gives a slightly lower figure for Jäskis, i.e. 252 (convictions). See Olli Matikainen, *Verenperijät: Väkivalta ja yhteisön murros itäisessä Suomessa 1500–1600-luvulla* (Helsinki, 2002), pp. 206–210; KA, judicial district of Jäskis, Stranda and Äyräpää II, judgment books 1700–1707. Insubordination in the 1660s and 1670s (and the late 1690s) was at least partly due to crop failure. The peaks of civil disobedience coincided with the years of crop failure or immediately after them. This also suggests that recalcitrance at the time of the Great Northern War was caused not only by the increased labour requirements brought about by the war but also by economic problems making it necessary to produce tax revenue with a decreased labour force.

Civil disobedience during the Great Northern War was mostly limited, precisely the kind of everyday resistance that Scott describes. The peasants neglected their obligation to maintain roads and bridges and deserted from militia service. Disobedience mostly concerned the crown. Accordingly to judicial sources, peasant disobedience towards the nobility was rare and of limited scope, and this fact is not altered even though not all matters of this kind made it to court, and the landowners managed them with their own means.

War-time disobedience was so widespread that the crown could punish the culprits only from time to time, on a selective basis in campaigns. The crown and the peasants were in a never-ending struggle, in which neither part gained any greater benefits but could not give up for fear of eventual losses. The mass desertion of called-up militia troops did not stop the authorities from arranging repeated call-ups. In many areas, everyday resistance led to stalemate situations of no benefit to either the crown or the peasants. In any case, the peasants demonstrated to the crown and its local representatives their unwillingness to bear any more burdens than those already placed upon them. This message was well received by the provincial governors and made them act in the ways described above.[243]

Disturbances of autocracy, including peasant insubordination and the concept, accepted in society from the top level all the way down, of the correspondence of the rights and obligations of each class and individuals thus prevent the crown from increasing the tax burden in any essential manner (except for having the taxes produced by a smaller workforce than before).

According to Eli F. Heckscher, England was able to treble crown revenue in the years 1700–1712/13 to respond to the challenges of war.[244] Walter Ahlström has demonstrated that in 1713 Sweden

---

[243] Kujala, *Miekka ei laske leikkiä*, pp. 83–155; Kujala, 'The Breakdown of a Society,' pp. 69–86.

[244] Eli F. Heckscher, 'De europeiska staternas finanser på Karl XII:s tid,' *Karolinska förbundets årsbok* 1921, pp. 59–66; Heckscher, *Sveriges ekonomiska historia från Gustav Vasa*, I:2, pp. 288–298.

and Finland, with conquered territories excepted had approximately as much regular and extra crown revenue at their disposal as in 1699, on the eve of the war. Ahlström sought to prove that the state economy was not launched into a downward spiral by the war. Moreover, his results show that Sweden could not improve taxation in the manner of England.[245] Economically undeveloped Sweden naturally could not afford the same stringent measures as England could, but in view of Sweden's precarious situation surrounded by hostile neighbours, it could have been expected to take slightly more active measures to improve war-time finances. Explanations for this failure to do so have been presented above.

The end result was that by the time that the Russians landed with superior numbers of troops on the shores of South Finland in May 1713, the supply of the Swedish army in Finland had been neglected so thoroughly that there were stores for only approximately one month. This was the case even though in the core areas of Finland, in the provinces of Åbo and Björneborg and Nyland and Tavastehus, there was enough grain to pay taxes and to supply the army, and an exceptionally good crop was even on its way.

With supply in a catastrophic state and with incompetent leadership the army in Finland failed almost completely to defend the country, and by early autumn it had given up the main areas of the country, Nyland and Finland-Proper, without any serious military opposition. Seeing that the army did not do its duty, i.e. defend the country and its inhabitants, the peasants ceased to pay taxes and to assist it. As the crown did not carry out its obligation of defending its subjects, the latter turned their backs on it, with truly serious consequences. The war effort was compromised even more and growing numbers of soldiers began to desert. For these reasons, national defence and civilian

---

[245] Ahlström, *Arvid Horn och Karl XII 1710–1713*, pp. 73–99. On the mistake in Ahström's calculation, which, however, does not alter his results in any essential manner, see Kujala, 'Why Did Finland's War Economy Collapse during the Great Northern War?', p. 84.

The Russians besieging and occupying Viborg in 1710 according to a Russian engraving. In the battle of Poltava in 1709 Tsar Peter the Great inflicted a heavy defeat on King Charles XII. The king remained isolated in Turkey for years. In 1710 the Russians conquered the last Baltic fortresses still in Swedish hands and Viborg, and took Finland in 1713–1714. Peter's plan was to keep the Baltic provinces and Viborg, if feasible, but Finland was in his mind no more than a pledge that could be utilised to force Sweden into a peace treaty that pleased Russia. As the Swedes did not get the message, the Russians destroyed Swedish coastal areas towards the end of the war. Peter was far too prudent to attack the heartland of the enemy, as Charles had done in 1708–1709. After returning from Turkey, Charles scraped the bottom of the barrel to attack Norway in 1718 but he fell during the early days of this campaign. National Board of Antiquities.

administration were on the brink of collapse. In many areas the common people and elements of the upper classes voluntarily submitted to enemy rule. The medieval conception of a system of mutual obligations linking those in power with their subjects was thus still in force.[246]

Sweden proper was spared a massive Russian invasion, but Martin Linde has demonstrated that here, too, the payment of taxes did not proceed well in 1713. According to him, there was a crisis of legitimacy in Sweden at the time.[247] Precisely the same phenomenon can be said to have existed in Finland in 1713, but in much more acute form. In this exceptional situation the peasants showed how much power they wield at most if the operations of society and the political system did not correspond in any way to their expectations and its legitimacy crumbled in their eyes.

CONCLUSIONS

The exceptional state of affairs of 1713 shows even more clearly than before that 17th-century society was not based on coercion alone but to an equal degree and even more on the fact that it enjoyed some kind of legitimacy even in the eyes of the common people. Laws, agreements, beliefs and institutions, including the principle of reciprocity and participation in the wielding of power, maintained this legitimacy. Although the peasants had less rights and more obligations than other estates in society they were not solely the supplying party in society, but also partner who had at least minor interests to defend. For them, these interests were not minor, for they had nothing else.

The Swedish nobility, which in international terms was weak, could never afford not to take the peasants completely into account. Attempts to intensify the manor economy and the control of the peasants remained modest even in comparison with

---

[246] Kujala, *Miekka ei laske leikkiä*, pp. 282–331. The same points are also discussed in my above-mentioned articles in English.

[247] Martin Linde, *Statsmakt och bondemotstånd: Allmoge och överhet under stora nordiska kriget* (Uppsala, 2000), pp. 190–200. Further studies on the war-time state and war economy of Sweden proper and the state of the population are needed in order to know the depth of the crisis in the core areas of the realm.

Denmark and more so when compared with Eastern Europe. The autocracy of Charles XI acted as if it did not have to give any thought to the upper classes or the peasants alike, but this situation proved to be only temporary. The emergence of autocracy was largely due to the need to intensify the use of the resources of society in case of war, but in reality autocracy functioned well only in peacetime.

In the situation caused by the war, the autocracy of Charles XII could not maintain the one-sided system of command, nor command anything like 100% support from the society for the king's war policies. Instead, the burdens caused by the war aroused widespread opposition. The interaction that now appeared in society was primarily negative for the government, but the government and crown authorities had no means to rectify the situation. Autocracy could not rise above society, and finally it fell down to ground level. When the king who had stubbornly continued the war died in battle in 1718, the autocratic system, which had arrived in a complete impasse had to join its master. It was replaced by the rule of the (higher) estates.

List of tables

List of diagrams

List of maps

Sources and bibliography

Unpublished sources

Kansallisarkisto (KA), Helsinki [National Archives of Finland]
Karl XI:s registratur (avskrift)
Karl XII:s registratur (avskrift)
Kungliga plakater och förordningar
Province accounts and their general documents
Sjundby gårds arkiv
Topographica II
Judgment books:
Judicial district of Jäskis, Stranda and Äyräpää II
    Lower Satakunta I–II
    Masku and Vemo
    Vemo and Lower Satakunta I–II

Krigsarkivet, Stockholm [Military Archives of Sweden]
Amiralitetskollegiet, kansliet

Lunds universitetsbibliotek (LUB)
De la Gardieska arkivet, Topographica,
    Harviala, Nokia & Hitå
    Kumo

Riksarkivet (RA), Stockholm [National Archives of Sweden]
Bielkesamlingen,
    Gustav Horn och Sigrid Bielke, Brev från underhavande på finska
    gods & Gods- och länshandlingar, Björneborgs grevskap och Vam-
    pula gård, Esbo & Meltola
    Nils Bielke och Eva Horn, Godshandlingar, Björneborgs grevskap
Brahesamlingen, Per Brahe d.y., Finska godshandlingar, Juva (S:t Mår-
    tens) & Pargas
Kammarkollegium till Kungl. Maj:t
Landshövdingars skrivelser till K.M:t, Åbo och Björneborgs län, Ny-
    lands och Tavastehus län, Österbottens län
Rådets registratur
Barthold Ruuths arkiv, Godshandlingar, Nylands och Tavastehus län
Rydboholmssamlingen
    Brev till Per Brahe d.y
    C. G. Wrangels ekonomiska brevväxling.

192

Wrangelska godshandlingar, Bjärnå
Sävstaholmssamlingen I
Tottska samlingen, Clas Tott, Godshandlingar, Gerknäs & Sjundby
Wijksamlingen, Gustav Horn och Sigrid Bielke, Ankomna brev
Kammararkivet:
Grev- och friherreskap, Kajana & Vasaborg
Kammarkollegiet, Generalbokhålleriet, Rikshuvudböcker
Kamreraren D. Norbergs kontor
Länsräkenskaper
Reduktionskollegii akter

Printed sources

Gahm-Persson, S. L. (ed.), *Kongl. Stadgar, Förordningar, Bref och Re-solutioner Angående Svea Rikes Landt-Milice*, I–IV (Stockholm, 1762–1814)
De la Gardiska Archivet, 13 (Lund, 1840)
Historiska handlingar, 5 & 7 (Stockholm, 1866, 1870)
Schmedeman, J. (ed.), *Kongl. Stadgar, Förordningar, Bref och Resolu-tioner Ifrån Åhr 1528 in til 1701 Angående Justitiae och Executions-Ährender* (Stockholm, 1706)
Stiernman, A. A. (ed.), *Alla Riksdagars och Mötens Besluth*, II–III (Stock-holm, 1729, 1733)
Stiernman, A. A. von (ed.), *Samling utaf Kongl. Bref, Stadgar och Fö-rordningar Angående Sveriges Rikes Commerce, Politie och Oeco-nomie*, II–V (Stockholm, 1750–1766)
Styffe, C. G. (ed.), *Samling af instructioner för högre och lägre tjenste-män vid Landt-Regeringen i Sverige och Finnland* (Stockholm, 1852)

Bibliography

Aalto, Seppo, *Kirkko ja kruunu siveellisyyden vartijoina: Seksuaalirikol-lisuus, esivalta ja yhteisö Porvoon kihlakunnassa 1612–1700* (Hel-sinki, 1996)
Åberg, Alf, *Karl XI* (Falun, 1994)
Ahlström, Walter, *Arvid Horn och Karl XII 1710–1713* (Lund, 1959)
Ågren, Kurt, *Adelns bönder och kronans: Skatter och besvär i Uppland 1650–1680* (Uppsala, 1964)
Ågren, Sven, *Karl XI:s indelningsverk för armén: Bidrag till dess histo-ria åren 1679–1697* (Uppsala, 1922)

Allardt, Anders, *Borgå sockens historia*, I (Helsingfors, 1925)

Anderson, Perry, *Lineages of the Absolutist State* (London, 1977)

Ardent, Gabriel, 'Financial Policy and Economic Infrastructure of Modern States and Nations,' *The Formation of National States in Western Europe*, Charles Tilly (ed.) (Princeton, 1975)

Ardent, Gabriel, *Histoire de l'impôt*, I–II (Fayard, 1971–1972)

Åström, Sven-Erik, *From Stockholm to St. Petersburg: Commercial Factors in the Political Relations between England and Sweden 1675–1700* (Helsinki, 1962)

Åström, Sven-Erik, 'The Role of Finland in the Swedish National and War Economies during Sweden's Period as a Great Power,' *Scandinavian Journal of History* 1986

Åström, Sven-Erik, 'Suurvalta-ajan valtiontalous,' *Suomen taloushistoria*, 1 (Helsinki, 1980)

Axelson, Gustaf Edvard, *Bidrag till kännedomen om Sveriges tillstånd på Karl XII:s tid* (Visby, 1888)

Beik, William, *Urban Protest in Seventeenth-Century France: The Culture of Retribution* (Cambridge, 1997)

Benedict, Ruth, *The Crysanthemum and the Sword* (Tokyo, 1954)

Bercé, Yves-Marie, *Histoire des Croquants* (Paris, 1986)

Blickle, Peter, *Der Bauernkrieg: Die Revolution des Gemeinen Mannes* (München, 1998)

Blickle, Peter, *Unruhen in der ständischen Gesellschaft 1300–1800* (München, 1988)

Bloch, Marc, *Feudal Society*, 1–2 (Chicago, 1993)

Blomstedt, Yrjö, *Laamannin- ja kihlakunnantuomarinvirkojen läänittäminen ja hoito Suomessa 1500- ja 1600-luvuilla (1523–1680)* (Helsinki, 1958)

Bonsdorff, Johan Gabriel von, *Stor-Furstendömet Finlands kameral-lagfarenhet*, I–II (Helsingfors, 1933)

Brenner, Alf, *Sjundeå sockens historia*, I (Hangö, 1953)

Brunner, Otto, *Land und Herrschaft: Grundfragen der territorialen Verfassungsgeschichte Österreichs im Mittelalter*, 5. Aufl. (Darmstadt, 1990)

Burke, Peter, *History and Social Theory* (Polity Press, 1998)

Carlsson, Sten & Rosén, Jerker, *Svensk historia*, I (Stockholm, 1964)

Cubero, José, *Une révolte antifiscale au XVIIe siècle: Audijos soulève la Gascogne (1664–1675)* (Paris, 2001)

Dahlgren, Stellan, 'Ekonomisk politik och teori under Karl XI:s regering,' *Karolinska förbundets årsbok 1998*

Dahlgren, Stellan, *Karl X Gustav och reduktionen* (Uppsala, 1964)

Dahlgren, Stellan, 'Karl XI,' *Kungar och krigare* (Stockholm, 1993)

Danielsen, Rolf et al., *Norway: A History from the Vikings to Our Own Times* (Oslo, 1995)

Det danske godssystem – udvikling och afvikling 1500–1919, Carsten Porskrug Rasmussen et al. (eds) (Århus, 1987)

Davis, Natalie Zemon, *The Gift in Sixteenth-Century France* (Madison, 2000)

Duby, Georges, *The Three Orders: Feudal Society Imagined* (Chicago, 1980)

Ekeberg, Birger, *Om frälseränta: En rättshistorisk utredning* (Stockholm, 1911)

Elgenstierna, Gustaf (ed.), *Den introducerade svenska adelns ättartavlor*, I–IX (Stockholm, 1925–1936)

Eng, Torbjörn, *Det svenska väldet: Ett konglomerat av uttrycksformer och begrepp från Vasa till Bernadotte* (Uppsala, 2001)

Englund, Peter, *Det hotade huset: Adliga föreställningar om samhället under stormaktstiden* (Stockholm, 1994)

Englund, Peter, *Ofredsår* (Stockholm, 1993)

Englund, Peter, *Den oövervinnerlige* (Stockholm, 2000)

Ernby, Eibert, *Adeln och bondejorden: En studie rörande skattefrälset i Oppunda härad under 1600-talet* (Uppsala, 1975)

Fuller, William C., *Strategy and Power in Russia, 1600–1914* (New York, 1992)

Gardberg, John, *Kimito friherreskap: En studie över feodal läns- och godsförvaltning* (Helsingfors, 1935)

Goubert, Pierre, *Les paysans français au XVIIe siècle* (Hachette, 1994)

Gurevitsj, A. Ja., 'De frie bønder i det føydale Norge,' *Frihet og føydalisme: Fra sovjetisk forskning i norsk middelalderhistorie*, Steinar Supphellen (ed.) (Oslo, 1977)

Gustafsson, Harald, 'The Conglomerate State: A Perspective on State Formation in Early Modern Europe,' *Scandinavian Journal of History* 1999

Gustafsson, Harald, *Political Interaction in the Old Regime: Central Power and Local Society in the Eighteenth-Century Nordic States* (Lund, 1994)

Gutsherrschaft als soziales Modell: Vergleichende Betrachtungen zur Funktionsweise frühzeitlicher Agrargesellschaften, Jan Peters (ed.), Historische Zeitschrift, Beiheft 18 (München, 1995)

Haggrén, Georg, *Hammarsmeder, masugnsfolk och kolare: Tidigindustriella yrkesarbetare vid provinsbruk i 1600-talets Sverige* (Pieksämäki, 2001)

Haikari, Janne, *Suurläänitys – perintötilallisen uhka?: Läänityslaitos Huittisissa 1638–1679*, unpublished MA thesis in Finnish history, University of Jyväskylä 1999

Heckscher, Eli F., 'De europeiska staternas finanser på Karl XII:s tid,' *Karolinska förbundets årsbok* 1921

Heckscher, Eli F., *Sveriges ekonomiska historia från Gustav Vasa*, I:2 (Stockholm, 1936)

Heino, Ulla, *Eurajoen historia*, I (Jyväskylä, 1987)

Histoire des populations de l'Europe, Jean-Pierre Bardet & Jacques Dupâquier (eds) (Fayard, 1997)

Hormia, Yrjö, *Pyhämaan-Pyhärannan 300-vuotisvaiheita* (Rauma, 1939)

Huhtamies, Mikko, *Sijaissotilasjärjestelmä ja väenotot: Taloudellis-sosiaalinen tutkimus sijaissotilaiden käytöstä Ala-Satakunnan väenotoissa vuosina 1631–1648* (Helsinki, 2000)

Istoriia Norvegii (Moskva, 1980)

Istoriia Shvetsii (Moskva, 1974)

Jansson, Torkel, *Agrarsamhällets förändring och landskommunal organisation: En konturteckning av 1800-talets Norden* (Uppsala, 1987)

Jespersen, Knud J. V., *Danmarks historie*, 3 (København, 1989)

Jokipii, Mauno, 'Porin kreivikunta,' *Historiallinen Arkisto* 54 1953

Jokipii, Mauno, *Satakunnan historia*, IV (s.l., 1974)

Jokipii, Mauno, *Suomen kreivi- ja vapaaherrakunnat*, I–II (Helsinki, 1956, 1960)

Jutikkala, Eino, *Bonden – adelsmannen – kronan: Godspolitik och jordegendomsförhållanden i Norden 1550–1750* (København, 1979)

Jutikkala, Eino, *Bonden i Finland genom tiderna* (Helsingfors, 1963)

Jutikkala, Eino, 'Finlands befolkning och befolkande,' *Historisk Tidskrift för Finland* 1987

Jutikkala, Eino, *Läntisen Suomen kartanolaitos Ruotsin vallan viimeisenä aikana*, I–II (Helsinki, 1932)

Jutikkala, Eino, 'Suurien sotien ja uuden asutusekspansion kaudet,' *Suomen taloushistoria*, 1

Jutikkala, Eino, 'Väestö ja yhteiskunta,' *Hämeen historia*, II:1 (Hämeenlinna, 1957)

Jutikkala, Eino with Pirinen Kauko, *A History of Finland* (Espoo, 1984)

Kansallinen elämäkerrasto, I–V (Porvoo, 1927–1934)

Karlsson, Åsa, *Den jämlike undersåten: Karl XII:s förmögenhetsskatt 1713* (Uppsala, 1994)

Karonen, Petri, *Pohjoinen suurvalta: Ruotsi ja Suomi 1521–1809* (Porvoo, 1999)

Katajala, Kimmo, *Nälkäkapina: Veronvuokraus ja talonpoikainen vastarinta Karjalassa 1683–1697* (Helsinki, 1994)

Katajala, Kimmo, *Suomalainen kapina: Talonpoikaislevottomuudet ja poliittisen kulttuurin muutos Ruotsin ajalla (n. 1150–1800)* (Helsinki, 2002)

Kaukovalta, Kyösti, *Uudenkaupungin historia*, I (Tampere, 1917)

Kirby, David, *Northern Europe in the Early Modern Period: The Baltic World 1492–1772* (London, 1993)

Kirby, David, 'The Royal Navy's Quest for Pitch and Tar during the Reign of Queen Anne,' *Scandinavian Economic History Review* 1974

Kling, Eero, *"Stormechtigste Konungh, Allernådigste Herre": Rahvaan valitukset 1600–1680, lähitarkastelussa Vehmaan kihlakunta ja Vaasaporin kreivikunta*, unpublished MA thesis in Finnish history, University of Helsinki 2000

Koivisto, Olavi, *Laitilan historia*, I (Vammala, 1969)

Kuisma, Markku, *Helsinge sockens historia*, II (Jyväskylä, 1992)

Kuisma, Markku, *Metsäteollisuuden maa: Suomi, metsät ja kansainvälinen järjestelmä 1620–1920* (Helsinki, 1993)

Kujala, Antti, 'The Breakdown of a Society: Finland in the Great Northern War 1700–1714,' *Scandinavian Journal of History* 2000

Kujala, Antti, 'Karl XII, rådet och Finland 1700–1713,' *Historisk Tidskrift för Finland* 1999

Kujala, Antti, 'Kronan, adeln och bönderna i sydvästra Finland 1640–1700,' *Historisk Tidskrift för Finland* 2002

Kujala, Antti, *Miekka ei laske leikkiä: Suomi suuressa pohjan sodassa 1700–1714* (Helsinki, 2001)

Kujala, Antti, 'Subordinate to the Nobility and to Swedish Absolutism: The Peasantry of Finland 1630–1713,' *Rossiiskaia istoricheskaia mozaika / Russian Historical Mosaic*, Festschrift for John Keep (Kazan, 2003)

Kujala, Antti, 'Talonpoikien veronmaksukyvyn kehitys Turun ja Porin sekä Uudenmaan ja Hämeen lääneissä 1694–1712,' *Historiallinen Aikakauskirja* 1999

Kujala, Antti, 'Why Did Finland's War Economy Collapse during the Great Northern War?,' *Scandinavian Economic History Review* 2001

Kujala, Antti & Malinen, Ismo, 'Brottslighet mot liv i Finland i början av 1700-talet,' *Historisk Tidskrift för Finland* 2000

Kuvaja, Christer, *Försörjning av en ockupationsarmé: Den ryska arméns underhållssystem i Finland 1713–1721* (Åbo, 1999)

Kuvaja, Christer, 'Isonvihan verot: Sääntöjä vai mielivaltaa?,' *Verotushistoriaa*, 2 (Turku, 2000)

Kuvaja, Christer & Rantanen, Arja, *Sibbo sockens historia*, 1 (Jyväskylä, 1994)

Lappalainen, Jussi T., *Kaarle X Kustaan Venäjän-sota v. 1656–1658 Suomen suunnalla* (Jyväskylä, 1972)

Lappalainen, Jussi T., *Sadan vuoden sotatie: Suomen sotilaat 1617–1721*

(Helsinki, 2001)

Lappalainen, Mirkka, 'Släkt och stånd i bergskollegium före redukti-onstiden,' *Historisk Tidskrift för Finland* 2002

Lappalainen, Mirkka, 'Suosio, suoja ja sosiaalinen nousu,' *Historiallinen Aikakauskirja* 2002

Linde, Martin, *Statsmakt och bondemotstånd: Allmoge och överhet under stora nordiska kriget* (Uppsala, 2000)

Lindegren, Jan, 'Karl XII,' *Kungar och krigare*

Lindegren, Jan, 'Maktstatens resurser,' *Skiss till maktstatsprojekt* (Åbo, 1987)

Lindegren, Jan, 'Ökade ekonomiska krav och offentliga bördor 1550–1750,' *Lokalsamfunn og øvrighet i Norden ca. 1550–1750*, H. Winge (ed.) (Oslo, 1992)

Lindegren, Jan, 'Den svenska militärstaten 1560–1720,' *Magtstaten i Norden i 1600-tallet og dens sociale konsekvenser*, Erling Ladewig Petersen (ed.) (Odense, 1984)

Lindegren, Jan, Utskrivning och utsugning: *Produktion och reproduktion i Bygdeå 1620–1640* (Uppsala, 1980)

Lindeqvist, K. O., *Isonvihan aika Suomessa* (Porvoo, 1919)

Lindström, Johan Adolf, 'Kumo Socken uti historiskt hänseende,' *Suomi*, XX (1860)

Litzen, Veikko, *Perniön historia*, 1 (Salo, 1980)

Luukko, Armas, *Etelä-Pohjanmaan historia*, III (Vaasa, 1945)

Luukko, Armas, *Suomen historia 1617–1721* (Porvoo, 1967)

Mäkelä, Anneli, *Hattulan kihlakunnan ja Porvoon läänin autioituminen myöhäiskeskiajalla ja uuden ajan alussa* (Helsinki, 1979)

Mäntylä, Ilkka, 'Kronan och undersåtarnas svält,' *Karolinska förbundets årsbok* 1988

Mäntylä, Ilkka, *Kruunu ja alamaisten nälkä: 1690-luvun katovuosien verotulojen vähennys Pohjanmaalla ja esivallan vastatoimet* (Oulu, 1988)

Mäntylä, Ilkka, 'Suurvaltakausi,' *Suomen historian pikkujättiläinen* (Porvoo, 1987)

Matikainen, Olli, *Verenperijät: Väkivalta ja yhteisön murros itäisessä Suomessa 1500–1600-luvuilla* (Helsinki, 2002)

Matinolli, Eero, 'Kruununverotus,' *Varsinais-Suomen historia*, VI:4 (Turku, 1976)

Melander, K. R. & G., 'Katovuosista Suomessa,' *Oma Maa*, V (Porvoo, 1924)

Moon, David, *The Russian Peasantry 1600–1930* (London, 1999)

Moore, Barrington Jr., *Injustice: The Social Bases of Obedience and Revolt* (London, 1978)

Muroma, Seppo, *Suurten kuolovuosien (1696–1697) väestönmenetys Suomessa* (Helsinki, 1991)

Myrdal, Janken, *Jordbruket under feodalismen 1000–1700* (Borås, 1999)

Nikander, Gabriel & Jutikkala, Eino, *Säterier och storgårdar i Finland*, II (Helsingfors, s.a.)

Nilsson, Sven A., *De stora krigens tid: Om Sverige som militärstat och bondesamhälle* (Uppsala, 1990)

Nordin, Jonas, *Ett fattigt men fritt folk: Nationell och politisk självbild i Sverige från sen stormaktstid till slutet av frihetstiden* (Eslöv, 2000)

Norges historie, Knut Mykland (ed.), 7 (Oslo, 1977)

Oja, Aulis, *Marttilan pitäjän historia*, I (Forssa, 1959)

Olander, Gunnar, *Studier över det inre tillståndet i Sverige under senare tiden av Karl XII:s regering, med särskild hänsyn till Skaraborgs län* (Göteborg, 1946)

Oredsson, Sverker, 'Karl XII,' *Tsar Peter och kung Karl: Två härskare och deras folk* (Stockholm, 1998)

Orrman, Eljas, *Bebyggelsen i Pargas, S:t Mårtens och Vemo socknar i Egentliga Finland under senmedeltiden och på 1500-talet* (Helsingfors, 1986)

Orrman, Eljas, 'Säteribildningen i Finland under 1600-talet,' *Kustbygd och centralmakt 1560–1721* (Helsingfors, 1987)

Orrman, Eljas, *Säterien muodostus ja häviäminen Etelä-Suomessa 1600-luvulla*, unpublished MA thesis in Finnish history, University of Helsinki 1969

Österberg, Eva, 'Bönder och centralmakt i det tidigmoderna Sverige: Konflikt – kompromiss – politisk kultur,' *Scandia* 1989

Österberg, Eva & Sandmo, Erling, 'Introduction,' *People Meet the Law*, E. Österberg & S. Sogner (eds) (Otta, 2000)

Paaskoski, Jyrki, *Vanhan Suomen lahjoitusmaat 1710–1826* (Helsinki, 1997)

Papunen, P., *Rauman seudun historia*, I (Rauma, 1959)

Perniö – kuninkaan ja kartanoiden pitäjä (Helsinki, 1997)

Petitions in Social History, Lex Heerma van Voss (ed.), International Review of Social History, Supplement 9 (Cambridge, 2001)

Polanyi, Karl, *The Great Transformation: The Political and Economic Origins of Our Time* (Boston, 1957)

Porchnev, Boris, *Les soulèvements populaires en France de 1623 à 1648* (Paris, 1963)

Porskrug Rasmussen, Carsten, 'Godssystemer i Sønderjylland fra 1500-til 1700-tallet,' *Bol og By* 1996

Pylkkänen, Ali, *Talonpojan vainiolta sotilaan ruokapöytään: Tilojen ja niiden verojen osoittaminen sotilaille ja heidän perheillensä Suo-*

messa 1636–1654 (Helsinki, 1996)

Raeff, Marc, *The Well-Ordered Police State: Social and Institutional Change through Law in the Germanies and Russia, 1600–1800* (New Haven, 1983)

Ramsay, August, *Esbo II: Esbo socken och Esbogård på 1600-talet* (Helsingfors, 1936)

Ranta, Raimo, *Viipurin komendanttikunta 1710–1721: Valtaus, hallinto ja oikeudenhoito* (Helsinki, 1987)

Reinholdsson, Peter, *Uppror eller resningar?: Samhällsorganisation och konflikt i senmedeltidens Sverige* (Uppsala, 1998)

Revera, Margareta, *Gods och gård 1650–1680: Magnus Gabriel De la Gardies godsbildning och godsdrift i Västergötland*, 1 (Uppsala, 1975)

Roberts, Michael, *The Swedish Imperial Experience, 1560–1718* (Cambridge, 1979)

Roos, John E., *Uppkomsten av Finlands militieboställen under indelningsverkets nyorganisation 1682–1700* (Helsingfors, 1933)

Rösener, Werner, *Peasants in the Middle Ages* (Cambridge, 1992)

Scott, James C., *Weapons of the Weak: Everyday Forms of Peasant Resistance* (New Haven, 1975)

Söderberg, Johan, 'En fråga om civilisering: Brottmål och tvister i svenska häradsrätter 1540–1660,' *Historisk Tidskrift* 1990

Sundberg, Kerstin, *Stat, stormakt och säterier: Agrarekonomisk utveckling och social integration i Östersjöområdet 1500–1800* (Lund, 2001)

Suomen historian kartasto, Eino Jutikkala (ed.), (Porvoo, 1959)

Suomen kulttuurihistoria, I (Porvoo, 1979)

Svenskt biografiskt lexikon

Swedlund, Robert, *Grev- och friherreskapen i Sverige och Finland: Donationerna och reduktionerna före 1680* (Uppsala, 1936)

Swenne, Hakon, *Svenska adelns ekonomiska privilegier 1612–1651* (Göteborg, 1933)

Thompson, E. P., *Customs in Common* (Harmondsworth, 1993)

Thoré, Anders, *Akademibondens plikt, universitetets rätt: Feodala produktionsförhållanden vid Uppsala universitets gods 1650–1790* (Uppsala, 2001)

Tilly, Charles, *Coercion, Capital, and European States, AD 990–1992* (Cambridge, MA, 1995)

Tornberg, Matleena, 'Ilmaston- ja sadonvaihtelut Lounais-Suomessa 1550-luvulta 1860-luvulle,' *Turun historiallinen arkisto* 44 1989

Turpeinen, Oiva, 'Suomen väestö 1638–1815 sekä vertailu Viroon,' *Ihmisiä, ilmiöitä ja rakenteita historian virrassa*, Professori Antero Heikkiselle 60-vuotispäivänä omistettu juhlakirja (Joensuu, 2001)

Upton, Anthony F., *Charles XI and Swedish Absolutism* (Cambridge, 1988)

Valpas, Risto, *Länsi-Suomen väestöolot suurista kuolovuosista Uuden-kaupungin rauhaan (1698–1721)*, unpublished licentiate study in Finnish and Scandinavian history, University of Helsinki 1965

Villstrand, Nils Erik, *Anpassning eller protest: Lokalsamhället inför utskrivningarna av fotfolk till den svenska krigsmakten 1620–1679* (Åbo, 1992)

Villstrand, Nils Erik, 'Stormaktstiden 1617–1721,' *Finlands historia*, 2 (Ekenäs, 1993)

Virrankoski, Pentti, 'Pohjois-Pohjanmaa ja Lappi 1600-luvulla,' *Pohjois-Pohjanmaan ja Lapin historia*, III (Oulu, 1973)

Vlastos, Stephen, *Peasant Protests and Uprisings in Tokugawa Japan* (Berkeley, 1990)

Ylikangas, Heikki, *Aikansa rikos – historiallisen kehityksen valaisijana* (Juva, 2000)

Ylikangas, Heikki, 'The Historical Connections of European Peasant Revolts,' *Scandinavian Journal of History* 1991

Ylikangas, Heikki, *Käännekohdat Suomen historiassa* (Porvoo, 1986)

Ylikangas, Heikki, *Klubbekriget: Det blodiga bondekriget i Finland 1596–97* (Stockholm, 1999)

Ylikangas, Heikki, *Lohjalaisten historia*, 1 (Helsinki, 1973)

Ylikangas, Heikki, *Mennyt meissä* (Porvoo, 1990)

Ylikangas, Heikki, 'What Happened to Violence?,' *Five Centuries of Violence in Finland and the Baltic Area* (Helsinki, 1998)

Yrjö Koskinen, (G. Z.,) 'Muutamia lisä-tietoja nälkä-vuosista 1695–1697,' *Historiallinen Arkisto* 1 1866

INDEX